Praise for *Ask More*

Deeply insightful, immediately practical, surprising, moving and entertaining all at the same time, Frank Sesno shows us how asking the right questions in the right ways empowers everyone—from famous figures like Colin Powell and Bill Gates to single moms struggling to raise families. One of the absolute essential skills of life, asking questions, as Sesno explains, can help us improve our relationships, find more success and satisfaction in our careers, and, perhaps most importantly of all, lead more fulfilling, interesting lives.

—Brian Baird, former Congressman (D-Washington)

Part memoir, part master class, Frank Sesno's *Ask More* draws on his own successes and failures as an interviewer as well as on discussions with an all-star cast to illustrate ways to best ask eleven types of questions ranging from confrontational ones to those creating a legacy. This is a must-read book both for those whose livelihood depends on securing answers to important questions and for those seeking the kinds of memorable conversations with family and friends that are facilitated by thoughtful queries.

—Kathleen Hall Jamieson, co-author *UnSpun: Finding Facts in a World of Disinformation.* Director of the Annenberg Public Policy Center at the University of Pennsylvania

Frank Sesno's book reveals one big secret of leadership: Top leaders use both emotional intelligence and facts to ask the right questions, get the information they need, and solve big problems.

—Farai Chideya, journalist, broadcaster, and author of books including *The Episodic Career: How to Thrive at Work in the Age of Disruption*

Using rich stories and practical takeaways, renowned journalist Frank Sesno shows us the surprising, powerful ways that questioning can improve our lives—and even our world.

—Warren Berger, questionologist and author of *A More Beautiful Question*

This book challenges us to take an expansive approach to problem-solving. Frank Sesno shows us how to diagnose a problem or identify an opportunity through incisive and sustained questioning. If we ask with diverse perspectives in mind, we can come up with even bigger and more innovative solutions.

—Susie Scher, Managing Partner, Goldman Sachs

Anyone who seeks good answers to important questions should read this book. In it, Sesno will teach you the art and science of posing superlative questions. Well written and carefully framed, I will certainly assign it to my students.

—Ernest Wilson, Dean of the Annenberg School for Communication and Journalism at the University of Southern California

We are living in a time of declarations and exclamation points. Our public sphere is often not a space of inquiry, but of accusation and polemic. How simple, and how refreshing, to be able to change the channel with Sesno's *Just Ask*. Its chapters are filled with ways to think about engaging others in a spirit of open, honest, inquiry—sometimes empathetic, sometimes confrontational, but always in the spirit of making our dialogues more constructive. Whether we are teachers, politicians, executives, plumbers, sons, daughters, spouses, or friends, Sesno reminds us that the art of the question is at the heart of who we are as human beings. A great read—peppered with compelling examples and moving stories of how questions, not answers, have the deeper power to change our world.

—Laurie Patton, President, Middlebury College

Frank Sesno has written an original, fast-moving and thought-provoking book about questions. But the secret is that this book is full of answers, too. From Colin Powell to Jorge Ramos, from an expert roofer to Sesno's disabled sister, you'll see how people put questions to work for them. You'll learn about the simple effectiveness of echo questions, and the power of questions without question marks. Read this book to deepen your own insights into life's most exciting challenges—how to learn, work, explore and ultimately, how to live. You might find, as I did, that the answers lie mostly in asking the right questions.

—Timothy Shriver, Chairman, Special Olympics

ASK MORE

ASK

The Power of Questions
to Open Doors,
Uncover Solutions,
and Spark Change

MORE

FRANK SESNO

AMACOM

AMERICAN MANAGEMENT ASSOCIATION
New York • Atlanta • Brussels • Chicago • Mexico City
San Francisco • Shanghai • Tokyo • Toronto • Washington, DC

Bulk discounts available. For details visit:
www.amacombooks.org/go/specialsales
Or contact special sales:
Phone: 800-250-5308
Email: specialsls@amanet.org
View all the AMACOM titles at: www.amacombooks.org
American Management Association: www.amanet.org

Library of Congress Cataloging-in-Publication Data
Names: Sesno, Frank, author.
Title: Ask more : the power of questions to open doors, uncover solutions,
    and spark change / by Frank Sesno.
Description: New York, NY : AMACOM, 2017.
Identifiers: LCCN 2016031122 | ISBN 9780814436714 (hardcover) | ISBN
    9780814436721 (ebook)
Subjects: LCSH: Interpersonal communication. | Questioning. | Decision making.
Classification: LCC BF637.C45 S474 2017 | DDC 650.1--dc23 LC record available
at https://lccn.loc.gov/2016031122

10 9 8 7 6 5 4 3 2

This book is dedicated to Kathy, my forever love; to our children Matt, Emily and Chris and daughter-in-law Emily, our future; and to Lora, our inspiration. Enjoy the journey, share it generously and never stop asking.

ACKNOWLEDGMENTS

I launched this project inspired by questions asked over a lifetime. Navigating the daunting challenges of writing a book, buffeted by the gusts of life and work, proved more difficult and more rewarding than I imagined. The project never would have made it out of my head had it not been for the help and encouragement of some of the most committed and creative people on the planet. First of all, my wife, Kathy, who believed in me and the book in ways that can only be called incredible. Whether it was the first question in the morning or the last word at night, she encouraged me as ideas evolved from concepts to chapters. She read with a dispassionate eye and edited with a steady hand. She made every page better.

The direction, counsel, and support of my agent, Steve Ross, helped launch the project and keep me focused. Steve offered insight and guidance that refined my thoughts and sharpened my approach. He navigated me through a sea I'd never sailed, always with a clear and confident eye.

My editor Ellen Kadin at AMACOM was a delight to work with. Her edits were precise. She challenged me, always in good ways, to write cleanly and clearly. She reassured me as I tilted at the calendar windmills and offered understanding when I needed more time.

ACKNOWLEDGMENTS

Seth Schulman helped me develop an arc and a conceptual approach. Jay Heinrichs parsed my words and told me when a chapter worked or, even better, when it did not.

The students in my Art of the Interview class convinced me there was a book here through their discoveries driven by their questions. The students who helped me with research, fact-checking, and editing were phenomenal. Nicholas Galbraith, Kristi Arbogast, Kate McCormick, you are amazing. Farida Fawzy, you will discover the world. Brent Merritt, thank you for your thoroughness, enthusiasm, and energy. You added horsepower to this project.

I owe my colleagues at The George Washington University and the School of Media and Public Affairs a debt of gratitude. They showed how an elegantly crafted question can blossom from research to revelation. My special thanks go to the infinitely committed Kim Gross, who bore the brunt of my fractured attention span as book deadlines loomed, and to the esteemed Robert Entman, whose research was a beacon and whose advice was invaluable.

I built this book around people who ask questions uncommonly well. Many of their stories made it into the text. Inevitably, some did not, though every conversation informed my writing. I wish I could have included everything. To all, I am deeply grateful. Your experience and your stories illuminated the ideas I was trying to convey. To Whit Ayers, Ed Bernero, Debbie Bial, Jim Buizer, Eve Burton, Dylan Byers, Jean Case, Adrienne Clair, Anderson Cooper, Al Darby, Jim Davis, Ken Doka, John Durham, Robert Entman, Tony Fauci, Nina Federoff, Gary Fink, Teresa Gardner, Terry Gross, Dave Isay, Rick Leach, Catherine Lee, Steve Miller, Gavin Newsom, Sandra Day O'Connor, Ted Olson, Diana Oreck, Karen Osborne, Colin Powell, Betty Pristera, Pradeep Ramamurthy, Jorge Ramos, Diane Rehm, Helen Riess, David Sanger, Bob Schieffer, Ed Scott, Jagadish Shukla, Barry Spodak, Shelly Storbeck, Sydney Trattner, Kevin Winston, Howard Zucker—thank you all for sharing your questions and your curiosity. The world is a much better place because you asked.

A personal thanks to Barbara Bradley Hagerty, who offered her experience as a journalist-author and insisted I could do this. Anne Rodgers kept the torch burning and helped light the way. Denise Schlener shared stories that showed how good questions cement good relationships. Chris Schroeder opened his home and hosted a remarkable dinner party that became a chapter in the book.

I am so deeply grateful to the place that gave me the opportunity to ask more questions and dig into more stories about the human condition than I ever could have imagined. I grew as a journalist as CNN grew from a cable experiment to a global presence. It was revolutionary then and it still is. Ted Turner, thank you on behalf of the planet for your vision and your guts. It wasn't easy. And to my friend Rick Davis, I will never be able to properly convey my appreciation for your undying guidance, friendship, and superb judgment in the years we worked together. You always had a better way to frame a question in search of a clear answer. Wolf Blitzer, you are a one-of-a-kind champion of journalism and accountability. I hope CNN never relinquishes its mission to inform and engage and take people to unexpected places where they meet new people, encounter new ideas, and consider new horizons.

Finally, I want to thank my children, Matt, Chris, and Emily, daughter-in-law Emily, and my sisters Lora and Julie. You are my points on the compass. You are gifts to the future. Stay curious.

CONTENTS

CONTENTS

CONTENTS

CONTENTS

FOREWORD

If you want answers, you have to ask questions.

It sounds simple. But it isn't. Asking the right question, at the right time, of the right person—and knowing what to do with the answer you get—takes thought, skill, practice and—sometimes—luck. As my friend and former colleague Frank Sesno explains in this inspired and inspiring book, questions can solve problems. They can change lives. And the right questions at the right moment can even influence history.

In the spring of 1977 a group of reporters shuffled into a small room on the first floor of Blair House, the brick townhouse on Pennsylvania Avenue across from the White House. Anwar Sadat, the President of Egypt, was staying there and had agreed to take questions from the media. Tension in the Middle East was high, but Sadat—erudite and savvy—seemed eager to open a new chapter in the region. A young reporter in the back of the room eventually raised his hand.

"Mr. President," he said, "you seem so sincere in your quest for peace. Why don't you do something to demonstrate that to Israel? Perhaps you could open some direct human contact with Israel? Why not allow an exchange of journalists or athletes or scholars?"

It seemed like a simple question, but it was one no one had asked. If you want peace, wouldn't there have to be face-to-face contact first?

Sadat thought for a minute. Then he answered: "Part of the Arab-Israeli conflict is a psychological one. I myself have no objection to this. But, believe me, our people are not yet ready for this after 29 years of hatred and four wars and bitterness. All that has happened . . .we must take it gradually."

I was the young reporter at the back of the room. And that question, Sadat would later say "germinated" in his mind for months, eventually leading to his groundbreaking trip to Jerusalem to address the Knesset, Israel's Parliament, and later, in 1979, to a peace treaty signed at the White House. For all the trouble in the region, that Israeli-Egyptian peace treaty remains in effect, a shred of stability in a volatile area.

There are few people in journalism better at asking questions than Frank Sesno. As CNN's White House Correspondent, Frank never shied away from speaking truth to power. He was smooth yet forceful, respectful but skeptical. He asked probing and sharp questions. There were no speeches in his questions, no grandstanding. He listened closely to the answers and he followed up when the White House dodged or tried to change the subject.

Later, as the host of CNN's Sunday talk show, Frank interviewed people from every walk of life. He questioned politicians and business leaders, Nobel Prize winners and celebrities, activists and athletes. He asked tough questions when necessary, but he could also gently draw out a guest who had suffered a setback, or been through tragedy. Frank's passion for engaging people and asking questions reflects his deep curiosity in others and their stories. It shines through in *Ask More*, as Frank shows how anyone can be more successful by asking questions more effectively.

When I came to CNN in 1990, my experience was as a print reporter. I wasn't used to my questions being seen on-camera or scrutinized by viewers. In those early days, Frank allowed me to shadow him as he worked. Later, when he was CNN's Washington Bureau Chief, I benefited from his advice and counsel as I formulated my own questions to ask presidents, kings, and dictators. Frank was not only a friend and mentor; he was an exceptional teacher (something he now does for a new generation at The George Washington University). His talent for getting to the heart of the matter and making fundamental concepts clear through compelling stories and vivid examples makes this a truly engaging book from which everyone will benefit.

There are different types of questions for different types of situations. Sometimes you're asking questions because you really don't know the answer; other times you need to confront a person in power to hold him or her to account. In *Ask More* Frank explains how questions differ and how they can be used to elicit information, educate your audience, explore untold stories, build bridges, and more. His insights and practical tips—from the types of questions to ask and the best ways to structure them, to suggestions for better listening—are useful in all aspects of life and will change the way you think about asking questions.

In *Ask More*, Frank shares real-world examples from fascinating people skilled in probing for answers to show how all of us can use the right questions to obtain information that might otherwise elude us, to solve difficult problems, to be more creative and better informed, or to make stronger human connections. *Ask More* can help anyone become a better learner, leader, innovator, or citizen. From the boardroom to the living room—and maybe even the White House briefing room—if you're looking for answers or inspiration, this book is for you. It will give you a deeper understanding of how questions work and the best ways to learn and succeed when you ask more.

Wolf Blitzer

CHAPTER 1

WHY ASK?

SMALL QUESTIONS MAKE SMARTER PEOPLE. We learn, connect, observe, and invent through the questions we ask. We push boundaries and we discover secrets. We solve mysteries and we imagine new ways of doing things. We ponder our purpose and we set our sights. We hold people accountable. We live generously, to paraphrase John F. Kennedy, by asking not what others can do for us, but what we can do for them. Curiosity opens our minds and captivates our imaginations.

But the fact is, most of us don't really understand how questions work—or how to make them work *for* us. In school we study math and science, literature and history. At work we learn about outcomes and metrics, profit and loss. But never do we study how to ask questions strategically, how to listen actively, or how to use questions as a powerful tool toward accomplishing what we really want to achieve.

Questions—asked the right way, under the right circumstances—can help you achieve both short-term and lifelong goals. They can open doors to discovery and success, bring you closer to a loved one, and even uncover answers to the universe's most enduring mysteries. Insightful questions help you connect with a stranger, impress a job interviewer, or entertain at your next dinner party, and they can be the keys to a happier, more productive, and fulfilling life.

This book shows you what you get when you ask for it. In each chapter I explore a different *type* of question, driven by its own approach and listening skills. By the end of the book, you'll be able to recognize what to ask and when, what you should listen for, and what you can expect as the outcome. Each chapter offers stories and looks at the genre through remarkable people who have used questions to motivate and excel.

For nearly four decades it's been my job to ask questions. From an inner-city school to a technology revolution, from the Brandenburg Gate where a president said, "Mr. Gorbachev, tear down this wall!" to the inauguration of the first African-American president, I have had the privilege of being there—watching, listening, and asking. I've interviewed world leaders who shaped history and heroes who dedicated themselves to the poor and the disabled. I've questioned avowed racists and the richest man in the world. As a journalist and interviewer, I have been enriched by these experiences and privileged to share them publicly—on CNN, NPR, and other media, and in front of live audiences. Now I teach college students how to ask to get information, to find the facts, to hold the powerful to account, and to create revealing moments for the world to see.

As my fascination with inquiry has grown, I've become increasingly alarmed about the questions we ask—or don't ask—in public and daily life. Technology has revealed endless horizons, but it has also created a quick-hit, search-engine culture where a fast answer can obscure deeper inquiry. The polarization of politics, amplified by social media, has fractured civic discourse and infused it with invective instead of dialogue. The news media, reflecting and reinforcing these trends, have grown shorter and sharper. Compared to when I got into the business, television interviewers are given less time and focus more on controversy and horse race than on explanation and substance. Sincere questions too often play second fiddle to certainty, ideology, and outrage. But what if we asked more and asserted less? What would we discover? How much better would we understand the people around us? What if we went asking for solutions and posed truly creative questions that could change the world?

A student convinced me I should write this book.

Simone (I've changed her name) had arranged to interview her father—I'll call him Morley—for an assignment I had given my Art of the Interview class. A devoted family man, Morley kept his emotions to himself and was not prone to reflection. At first he refused. "Go find someone else," he told his daughter. But Simone persisted, and finally her father agreed to the interview, camera and all.

Simone had questions she always wanted to ask. Morley had issues he never wanted to discuss. They sat facing each other in the den, a place both of them knew well. Simone started with some innocuous open-ended questions, a classic interviewing technique. She asked about her father's college days and how he met his wife, Simone's mother. When Morley seemed more relaxed, Simone asked the question she'd been thinking about for a long time.

"Before I was born a child passed away," she said. "Can you tell me what happened?" For more than twenty years, the family had faithfully commemorated the child's birthday, but they had never really talked about what happened.

"She was born premature," Morley said. "She lived for about a day and a half. Her lungs hadn't fully formed. That created a series of other problems." He paused. Then came the secret he'd never told anyone, not even his own parents.

"Your mom and I decided that we would disconnect her from life support." His voice trailed off. He swallowed hard, trying to stay in control.

Simone kept going. "Was it a difficult decision? How did you and mom handle that?" Her father teared up. So did she.

Morley's words came slowly. "At the time it was very hard . . . It was probably hardest to see some of our friends with kids at that time." Another pause. "But those experiences shape you." He looked at his daughter. He saw a beautiful and smart young woman—his legacy and his love. Still emotional, Morley told her she wouldn't be alive if that terrible event had not occurred.

Simone's head was spinning. To learn the details was difficult enough, but to see her strong, unshakable father so upset revealed a vulnerability she had never seen.

"I understand now, after what he had been through, why I meant so much to him," she told me later. "I understand why he has always made such an effort to spend time with me, to be there for important events in my life, to tell me how proud he is of me. Now when he gives me a hug I don't pull away as quickly. When I miss his call I make sure to try him back right away."

Simone uncovered a deep secret, discovered a different side of her dad, and changed the way she related to her father *simply because she asked.* More, much more, than an oral history came from her questions.

And so I began to explore the power of questions in their different forms.

I talked to dozens of people, master questioners if you will, to understand how they used questions in their lives and professions and to see what we could learn from them. The inquiry teachers in this book comprise some of the most fascinating and successful people I've met, some famous and some not so famous. The arc of their lives has been assisted by their ability to question the people and the world around them.

The book begins with a problem. If you've ever confronted something that's gone wrong, with time running out, you know that asking the right questions can make the difference between a good call and a catastrophic mistake. Chapter 2 introduces you to people who diagnose problems for a living: a nurse-practitioner in Appalachia, a renowned corporate turnaround artist, and my neighbor, the roofer. They're all experts at asking questions to pinpoint a problem so they can fix it. You'll see how you can zero in, listen hard, and draw on experience and instinct.

Chapter 3, "The General's Charge," shows you how to stand back and think big when the stakes are high and the outcome is unclear. Strategic questions ask about choices, risks, and consequences. They force you to challenge conventional wisdom and your own biases. They lead to better, clearer thinking and better planning when you're weighing big decisions. As General Colin Powell explained to me, great strategic questions can inform the hardest decisions, just as failing to ask the right questions can lead to disaster.

If you want to connect with someone, you will see how the experts do it as you read Chapter 4, "From the Inside Out." Empathetic questions can bring you closer to people you know or have just met. These questions help you become a better friend, colleague, partner, or family member. They lead to deeper understanding and discovery. You'll hear from a family therapist, a Harvard professor who teaches empathy, and from one of the best interviewers in America, NPR's Terry Gross.

Want to know a secret, maybe a dangerous one? In Chapter 5 you'll learn how careful, patient questioning can build a bridge to someone who *doesn't* want to talk to you. These bridging questions reach out to people who are wary, distrustful, and even hostile. You'll see how an expert in Dangerous Threat Assessment uses them to solve difficult, and sometimes volatile, human puzzles. He asks questions without question marks. Understanding how this is done will help you communicate, if not with terrorists, then at least with teenagers.

And if no bridge can be built? Chapter 6 will show you how you can use confrontational questions to hold people accountable for what they've done or said. While this kind of inquiry is often unpleasant, as I once discovered in a bizarre encounter, it does establish a record. Know what you're after, as Anderson Cooper explains. Be prepared for the consequences, as Jorge Ramos recounts. But as you will see, if you have the courage of your convictions, know what you're talking about, and can ask with precision, you can be a more formidable adversary.

How many times have you heard that you should think outside the box, be original, and take a chance? In Chapter 7 you'll realize you can get there through questions, not commands. If you want to get creative juices really flowing, ask people to imagine, to set their sights high, to pretend gravity doesn't exist. What do California Lieutenant Governor and former San Francisco Mayor Gavin Newsom and Hollywood television series creator Ed Bernero have in common? They both use questions to transport people to a place where they cannot fail.

In Chapter 8, "The Solvable Problem," you'll see how you can create a sense of purpose and mission through your questions and inspire people to pitch in, or maybe even write a check. You'll meet Karen Osborne, who has raised millions of dollars, and Rick Leach, who wants to feed the world. You can borrow from their approach to become your own pied piper. You'll discover surprising ways to improve listening, set common goals, and take concrete action.

Chapter 9 ventures into the unknown and the unexplained to see how scientific questions can solve the mysteries of the world. You will meet the doctor-researcher who threw himself at HIV/AIDS and Ebola when people were dying and the public was in panic. You'll also find inspiration and ideas you can apply in your own life.

Next come the money questions. You're trying to fill a job. You *want* the job. What you ask tests your compatibility and, just maybe, predicts the future. Chapter 10 shows you how these questions get asked—from both sides. You'll meet a CEO who goes for the team approach and a technology veteran who just might ask about your favorite aisle in the supermarket.

Entertaining questions can turn your boring dinner into a theater of wit and ideas and provocative conversation. Be your own talk show host. In Chapter 11, you'll learn ways to draw out memorable dialogue and keep the conversation moving, using ideas from one of the most engaging and curious people I've ever met. Invite Socrates to supper—if you dare. Serve this recipe at your next meal and you'll have everyone talking.

Finally, what does it all mean? Chapter 12 asks legacy questions that reveal your life story and craft an uplifting narrative of accomplishment and gratitude. These questions from the edge will help you step back and take stock of what you have done and the people you have known. Here, you meet the rabbi who gets asked about God's intentions and read the curious words of a twenty-five-year-old who questions her future. I introduce you to one of the bravest people I've ever met.

At the back of the book, I provide a guide that summarizes the question categories and their component parts, with a few ideas you can try to become a more effective questioner.

This book is not prescriptive. It doesn't *tell* you how to ask in every situation. But it does offer examples that demonstrate the power of questions and the benefits of deep, nuanced listening. The categories reflect a range of curiosity. As you will see, each enlists different asking skills in search of distinct outcomes. Humans are built to be curious, that much is in our DNA. This book illustrates how some of the most successful people have honed their curiosity and developed an ability to ask and to listen that has served them extraordinarily well.

Our questions reflect who we are, where we go, and how we connect. They help us learn and they help us lead because effective questioning marshals support and enlists others to join. After all, asking people to solve a problem or come up with a new idea turns the responsibility over to them. It says, "You're smart, you're valuable, you know what you're doing—what would *you* do about this problem?"

My aim in writing this book is to show you the power of questions and how it can be applied effectively and freely. Enjoy and learn from the exceptional questioners you meet here.

And then, ask more.

CHAPTER 2

SOMETHING'S NOT RIGHT
Diagnostic Questions

THERE ARE DAYS REPORTERS DREAD, but they come with the territory. A rumor, a phone call, and then a pit in your stomach, no matter how seasoned you are. A passenger jet has disappeared. Air traffic controllers lost contact with the crew. The plane vanished from radar screens. Airline and aviation authorities are racing to figure out what's gone wrong. So are we.

In the newsroom, we are scrambling, preparing to go on the air with the story. What exactly will we say? What do we know? Where will definitive information come from? And when? We deploy reporters. We're all over the FAA and the FBI and the airline. We're using new flight-tracking apps. We're working sources, contacting anyone who might have heard anything. We brace ourselves for the most perilous time in live TV—that period after something happens but before anyone in authority can confirm what actually happened. If we get it wrong, we spread misinformation, scare innocent people, and may even affect the actions of first responders. We tarnish our credibility and outrage our viewers.

A lot of our work will unfold in real time, right in front of the audience as we ask the questions that track what's going on and what went wrong.

What airline and flight number?
How many were on board?
When and where did it disappear?

These are the first harried questions we ask in those early, frenzied moments—the *who, what, when,* and *where* questions of a breaking story.

Was there mechanical trouble?
Was anyone on a watch list?
What did witnesses see?

We need to know what happened and what went wrong. Until those questions are answered, the rest of the story will remain a mystery.

What's the Problem?

Fortunately, most planes land safely, and life does not unfold in a TV newsroom. But our need to identify problems so we can act on them is an ingredient of daily existence. The reporter's rapid instinct, like the clinician's expertise in connecting symptoms to illness, is a skill you can develop and incorporate into your questioning to become better, faster, and more precise when you have to diagnose a problem. Whether it's a life-threatening condition or a leak in the basement, a pain in the shoulder or an issue at work, you have to figure out what the problem is before you can do anything about it. You have to ask the right questions, accept bad news, and roll with the unexpected to get the answers you need in a timely fashion.

Since human beings first stepped out of our caves, we realized that if we were to survive, we had to identify peril and then avoid or overcome it. That still holds true, although these days, with Wi-Fi in our caves, we often call the experts. Still, we can hone our skills so that our diagnostic questioning is sharper. We can be better questioners of the doctor or the mechanic or the boss when they think they have the answers to our problems. We can challenge our political leaders when they speak with certainty about a simple problem and an easy solution.

Diagnostic questioning is the ground floor of inquiry. It is the foundation on which other questions are built. It pinpoints a problem and provides a roadmap for a response.

> *What's wrong?*
> *How do we know?*
> *What are we not seeing?*
> *What should we do?*

Diagnostic questioning identifies a problem then burrows down to its roots, especially when those roots are not instantly obvious.

Your tooth is killing you. You go to the dentist. She asks where it hurts, when it hurts. When you chew? When you drink? She taps, pokes, and applies cold water till you leap out of the chair. Oh sorry, did that hurt? Yes, you grunt, through the junkyard that litters your palate. She says the problem is this *other* tooth. You're feeling "referred pain." An X-ray confirms it. A filling fixes it.

Your company recently introduced a new product. It isn't selling. Everyone thinks it's a flop. You're not so sure, so you hire some consultants to figure out what's going on. They conduct focus groups. They ask lots of questions about this product and similar ones. They discover that people actually like it and several of them say they'd buy it—if they knew about it. Turns out the marketing was the problem.

Diagnostic questions, whether they are directed at a company or a cavity, progress systematically to describe the problem and identify it.

Connect symptoms and specifics. Start with big, broad, what's-the-problem questions and then narrow down, zero in. Get past the generic to identify the symptoms and describe related observations in detail.

Ask for the bad. Don't duck the issues or avert your eyes. Ask direct questions in search of direct answers. It may get ugly, but if you want to fix a problem, you have to acknowledge it to deal with it.

Study history. Look back. Ask about similar experiences, events, and patterns. They provide a baseline. Look for similarities to other situations.

Ask again. The mere existence of a problem means there is something unknown or unanticipated. To be sure you're on solid ground, ask several times and several sources. Confirm and corroborate.

Challenge the expert. We rely on experts to diagnose our disease. But that doesn't mean they're right or that they're off the hook in explaining what's going on. Before you accept a diagnosis, ask what it is, what it means, and where it's coming from. And reserve the right to get another opinion.

"Miss Nosy"

The first step in diagnostic questioning involves knowing what you're dealing with. Teresa Gardner is an expert at that. She's been celebrated by her peers, which is how I heard about her and tracked her down, and she's been profiled on national television. Fearless, tireless and endlessly resourceful, Teresa works in one of the most impoverished parts of America.

A nurse practitioner who makes her rounds through the hills and hollows of the Appalachian Mountains in southwestern Virginia, Teresa deals with what she calls "human train wrecks." Many of the people here are poor and chronically ill. They lack access to jobs and healthcare. Unemployment rates in many areas are twice or more the national average. Many eat poorly, get inadequate exercise, and neglect themselves in the scramble to make ends meet.

"It's an area of desperate need. But the people here are such good people," Teresa told me. Most are hardworking and proud. "Our patients are some of the nicest people you'd ever meet. They're down on their luck," but, she confides, "sometimes we have trouble getting people to accept help."

They need the help. Residents in this part of Appalachia experience disproportionately high rates of heart disease, diabetes, and pulmonary disease. Some counties report twice the early death rates as the rest of the state. Teresa spends her days on the move. Responding to the bottomless pit of need, she took her practice on the road, in the early years driving around in a beat-up old Winnebago called the Health Wagon. Her patients often had not visited a medical professional in years. But Teresa welcomed them with open arms and warm spirit, examined them, listened to their stories, diagnosed their illness, and prescribed their medication.

She used her questions like a scalpel, short and sharp, to cut to a problem to identify and try to fix it. She started with open-ended questions to get people talking and to prompt a description of the problem.

How are you feeling?
What are your symptoms?
How long has it been like this?

Teresa asks her patients about a lot more—their work and their home, their families and their lives, how they're eating and what they're drinking. She listens for clues pointing to the root of the problem. As she asks, she brings instinct, experience, and expertise to bear. She's been practicing since she was young.

Teresa grew up in this part of the country, in Coeburn, Virginia. She shared a tiny room with her sister in the trailer that was the family home. Her father worked in the mines, her mother in a sewing factory. Her dad had a bad back, and some days the pain was so acute, he would fall out of his truck at the end of the day and crawl to the front door.

While the family didn't have much, they had more than many, and they helped where they could. Her grandmother, "Mamow," a plump woman who lived nearby, opened her home to feed and occasionally house sick neighbors, some suffering from tuberculosis. Teresa's mother took meals to the local hospital. Teresa volunteered at the hospital, too.

A curious child from the time she was little, Teresa peppered her mother with questions about how things worked, where they came from and why. She asked about places and people. Her mother nicknamed her "Miss Nosy." Teresa took her inquisitive nature to school. She recalls the day her sixth-grade teacher, Mr. Bates, drew a heart on the blackboard and started explaining how it had chambers and valves and pushed blood out and through the body. She was mesmerized and wanted to know more about how the heart worked. How did it know how much and how fast to pump? She developed an interest in science and started reading magazines, books, articles—anything she could find about medicine and biology.

She became the first in her family to go to college and ultimately earned a doctorate in nursing practice. Then she came home. She wanted to work in the place where she was raised and where she knew her help was needed.

The Mystery Patient

Trekking across this complex terrain of geography and human need, Teresa elicits vital information from people who are often reluctant to talk. Her warm Virginia accent softens her questions, but they are nonetheless deliberate and focused. Teresa expects a detailed description of what hurts and where. She seldom wastes time or words. Often the problem is buried deep.

Teresa pulled the Health Wagon into Wise, Virginia, shortly before lunch one day, and a woman climbed aboard. She was short and overweight and in her early twenties. As usual, the first question was big and open and warm. With a smile she asked:

How are you doing today?

Not well, the woman said. Her head hurt. She was feeling tired and weak. She felt confused, disoriented. Teresa asked about her past health issues. The woman said she'd suffered from high blood pressure, chronic weight issues, and diabetes.

Teresa suspected the woman was having a diabetic attack. Her questions grew more specific and urgent, homing in.

What medicines are you on? What dosage?

When was your last insulin injection and last meal?

What are your other symptoms?

How long have you had diabetes? Is it Type 1 or Type 2?

When was your last lab work?

What has your insulin regimen been for the past few days?

The answers came in short, hesitant responses. But they added up. A blood test confirmed it: The patient was suffering from hyperglycemia. The treatment for diabetes and high blood sugar is straightforward. Strict diet and carb counting. Insulin, closely monitored. Regular doctor visits. The patient failed on all counts. She was taking insulin but wasn't sure of the dose. She hadn't been to a doctor in two years. Teresa wanted to know what was going on and why.

"When we talked to her, it wasn't obvious at first," Teresa explained. "But parts of the story were familiar. She worked two jobs, about sixty hours a week, but neither provided health insurance."

Teresa asked the patient where her insulin was coming from. Hesitantly, the patient acknowledged that her father, retired military, was a diabetic, too. He got his insulin through the Veterans Administration. The patient paused again, looked down, and continued. They had been splitting it.

It was a shocking revelation, though Teresa had heard worse. Teresa spoke slowly and directly, telling her patient about the importance of monitoring herself and her diet, and the potentially deadly consequences of sharing her father's medication. She wrote a prescription and advised her patient how to get insurance coverage so she could pay for it.

Teresa's questions effectively identified symptoms and cause, allowing her to plan the best treatment going forward. For now, at least, this young woman and her father would get the medicine they needed to treat the disease they both confronted.

Bad News Is Good News

If you're going to be an effective diagnostic questioner, you have to embrace something a lot of people would prefer to avoid: bad news. Nurse practitioners like Teresa Gardner look for bad news. They collect information with one purpose: to diagnose a problem so they can treat it. They need to know what's wrong. Reporters are drawn to bad news, too; that's their job. If that plane went missing as a result of a security lapse or because the hydraulics failed, they want to expose the problem and break the story. They look for power that's been abused, money that's been wasted, and investments that are Ponzi schemes.

If you're going to ask "What's wrong?" then you have to embrace bad news. It's why Steve Miller, a renowned investor and corporate turnaround artist, was in such demand and paid so much money over the past three decades. His book, *The Turnaround Kid: What I Learned Rescuing America's Most Troubled Companies*, tells his story of looking for bad news. A veteran of the auto industry, Miller can spot a wreck a mile away.

> *Why is this company in so much trouble?*
> *Where do the problems originate?*
> *What isn't working?*

Miller asks for the bad, and then tries to outsmart it. He listens for explanations, not excuses. When a mutual friend offered to introduce us, I eagerly accepted and booked a trip to New York City to see him.

Miller cut his turnaround-kid teeth alongside legendary Chrysler CEO Lee Iacocca. Burdened by high labor costs, poor quality, and uninspiring design, Chrysler faced extinction when superior Japanese imports began flooding the American market. As Chrysler's financial answer man, Miller helped put together that historic federal bailout that saved the company. After a falling out with the charismatic Iacocca, Miller left Chrysler and went looking for other endangered corporate species. He helped rescue trash giant Waste Management. He led Bethlehem Steel through bankruptcy. He salvaged what he could of auto-parts manufacturer Delphi.

Miller's approach has always revolved around fast questions, fast answers, and decisive, often painful action. Time has never been on his side. Sprawled in his office on Park Avenue in Midtown Manhattan, Miller told me that when companies call, it's usually because their situation has gone "from troubled to desperate."

When he takes on a challenge, he brings a fiercely competitive survivor's instinct and an outsider's eye to the job. "I like to say I'm fearless and clueless." He starts by looking for the problem that was the core threat to the business. "I do not regard myself as the answer man," he says. "I am the question man . . ."

Typically, Miller spends the first few weeks meeting with people—encouraging them to tell him what's wrong, what doesn't work, where the brick walls are getting in the way. After he asks about the past, he wants to know how people see the future.

When did things start going wrong?
What have you learned?
How do you think we fix it?

He explained to me that his biggest professional challenge was as CEO of Delphi, the auto-parts behemoth that had once been part of General Motors. The Delphi Corporation was a $28 billion company, hemorrhaging money when Miller took it over in 2005. Ultimately, Miller took the company through Chapter 11. At the time it was the biggest bankruptcy in the history of the American auto industry. An ugly, nasty, and exceptionally painful process, at times it seemed there was nothing but bad news.

Delphi had grown into the biggest auto-parts maker in the United States. By the time Miller walked through the door, the company had diversified into too many side ventures. It had lost focus on its core products even as global competition got fierce. It was buckling under huge legacy costs of healthcare and union pensions that it inherited when General

Motors spun off the company six years earlier. It was paying unionized workers up to $75 an hour in wages and benefits. Workers could retire at age 48 and keep their healthcare for life. Whenever the company closed a factory, it paid laid-off workers indefinitely until they got another Delphi job, a policy that cost the company $400 million a year.

Miller told the *Wall Street Journal* at the time that labor costs were "roughly triple" what any other unionized American auto supplier had to pay. He wanted to know:

> *What got us into the ditch?*
> *What happened to the business plan?*

Over dinner at the Frankfurt Auto Show, Miller recalled, he asked Delphi's international corporate customers to critique their experiences. It didn't take many rounds of schnapps for the horror stories to start flowing. They complained that Delphi had become a plodding, distant, tangled, bureaucratic nightmare of a company to work with. Getting a new braking system to Mercedes-Benz, for example, required sign-off from multiple divisions in different countries. Decisions took forever. The supply chain was broken. It was no way to run a competitive business. "It meant we were paralyzed," Miller told me.

In his book Miller compared himself to a surgeon and described Delphi as a "desperate patient who waited too long to seek treatment." He concluded that major surgery was required. Five months after his arrival, Delphi filed for bankruptcy and began its painful reorganization. Miller closed twenty-one of twenty-nine factories, putting four out of ten workers out of their jobs. He forced major wage concessions on the United Auto Workers (UAW) and unloaded most of its legacy costs in worker healthcare and pensions. He moved the company away from manufacturing old-style, low-profit parts—chassis, brakes, hoses—and into high-tech electronics, navigation, and fuel systems.

Miller fumbled some public statements, making a difficult task even harder. He complained that Delphi couldn't afford to pay union workers $65 an hour and fund healthcare and other expensive benefits even as the company approved big bonuses for top executives. Hourly workers erupted. Miller faced protests and court challenges. As penance and a PR move, he cut his salary from $1.5 million to just $1. Still, when he looked out his window one day, he saw union protesters carrying signs that said, "Miller Isn't Worth a Buck."

But as a result of asking his "bad news" questions, Miller knew the situation was dire. He also knew the crisis extended beyond Delphi. General Motors and other companies depended on Delphi auto parts. If Delphi went under, it could take automakers down with it.

"My goal was to do minimal harm to the world's auto industry," he said. "Yes, we had come out of GM, but we sold parts to every automaker on the planet, without which no automaker could do much."

At tremendous cost to workers and his own public profile, Miller salvaged the company. The concessions he forced and the ripple effect it had through the industry prompted business writer Allan Sloane to give Miller credit for saving "what's left of the Detroit Three automakers."

If the problem is eliminated, can we survive?

Miller's "fearless and clueless" approach to asking about and acting on bad news did not make him popular. But as a surgeon working on a desperately sick patient, he lived by the idea that if you want to fix a serious problem, you have to go looking for it and cannot avert your eyes when you find it. For years after his experience at Delphi, Miller wrote notes to the people whose lives were shattered in the reorganization, explaining and apologizing.

Bad news comes with a price, and whether it's a business that's confronting impossible legacy costs or a patient who is in denial about her diabetes, looking for bad news is a necessary first step toward diagnosis and action.

History Is News, Too

News can be bad or it can be good, but history is forever. And history is part of diagnostic questioning. It provides clues and reveals patterns.

When did you first notice this?
How long has it been going on?
What was it like before?

Some of the most effective diagnostic questioners are history buffs. My neighbor, Al Darby, is one of the best. He's a roofer who specializes in slate roofs, copper gutters, and that tricky flashing that wraps around chimneys and keeps the water where it belongs when it rains: outside. He usually gets called when a homeowner finds water in a bedroom or a hallway, dripping down the wall or puddled on the floor. He starts by asking about the history of the house, the roof, and the water problem.

Does it leak every time it rains?
Does the leak always start when the rain begins?
Where do you see the first signs of the leak and has that changed over time?

Al knows how water behaves. He knows it can travel twelve or fourteen feet across a pipe or beam of wood before dripping into a puddle, so the puddle's location doesn't necessarily correspond to where the water came in. He looks for patterns over time. The more he learns, the more specific his questions become. History has made him a detective.

Have you ever repaired the roof?
What exactly have you done?
Does the water drip from the ceiling or down the wall?
Does it only leak when the wind blows?

If the leaks correlate with wind, it could be that something outside has come loose or broken, and the problem might not involve the roof at all. If a repair has been made, he wants to know what materials were used, when, and whether the neighbor's house is similar and if she's had any water problems. Only after finding out all he can does Al take a hose to the roof to imitate a rainstorm and duplicate the problem.

Al's diagnosis frequently surprises the homeowner. Windows are often the culprits; people leave them open or they're not properly caulked. Clogged gutters are frequent offenders; if water doesn't drain properly, it can come in through shingles or siding. Wood can rot in the valleys or low points of the roof. Many times, Al has put his finger right through rotten wood that's let the rain in.

Al asks about a leaky home like a curator asks about a fading manuscript. He knows it is a vulnerable thing, exposed to the elements against the relentless march of time. He wants to know what it's been through and how it's been handled. He finds clues in the past.

Al takes immense pride in his questioning. "I love it," he told me, "because I like helping people solve their problems. It's as simple as that."

Challenge the Expert

Gardner, Miller, and Darby are all experts. They put their curiosity and their knowledge to work by asking on-the-money questions that help them identify and treat a problem.

The expert you're dealing with could be a doctor or a roofer, a high-priced consultant or a friend down the street. But even if they have far more experience than you'll ever have, be prepared to ask them about their diagnosis. How did they reach it? What is it based on and what is the prognosis? Ask about their process, their experiences in similar situations, and your options, risks, and next steps. Questioning an expert can be daunting and difficult. But often it's necessary. I know it's not easy because I've been through it, very close to home.

What are you telling me?
What does this mean?
What aren't you telling me?

My mother hadn't been feeling well for a while. She hadn't been happy with her doctor, either. He seemed dismissive of her complaints and suggested her problem was indigestion or just changes that come with age. He didn't ask whether the sensation corresponded to meals, how it affected her digestion or what was different from how she'd felt in the past. Frustrated and angry, Mom found another doctor who questioned her thoroughly, listened carefully, and ordered tests.

I was on vacation when I spoke to Mom on the phone a couple of weeks later. She sounded fine at first, her usual assertive self. But after a few minutes, she took a breath. Now, don't worry, she said, but she'd gotten some bad news. The tests were back. She had ovarian cancer.

Before I could even react, she said the doctor was great; he had already scheduled surgery and she'd be going in a few weeks, shortly after I was back. Then there would be chemotherapy. She had confidence in her doctor, she said. Things would be fine.

Life had always been a roller coaster with my mother. She was smart, quick, always sure of herself, profane—there wasn't a swear word she didn't use—and the most opinionated person I've ever met. It didn't matter if she was speaking to a teacher or a plumber; she judged everyone and everything. She referred to herself with pride as the "toughest broad on the block." She bragged about her stubborn independence, which set the tone for just about every conversation she had.

Mom came through the surgery pretty well, though when the nurses came by to get her up and walking, she barked them out of her room. She'd get up when she was good and ready, she said, and she wasn't ready. This was not going to be easy. The doctor reported that he was pleased with the surgery. He'd removed as much of the cancer as he could. He wasn't the warmest guy on the planet and could be abrupt. During rounds he was in fast, out fast. But he had a solid reputation as a surgeon and, most important, Mom loved him. She called him "Dr. Blue Eyes."

But we had questions for the doctor. Lots of them.

What lies ahead?
Which chemo drugs will be most effective?
How will Mom feel?
What side effects should we expect?
What is life going to be like during treatment?
What are her chances of beating this?

Getting answers out of Doctor Blue Eyes was agonizing. He never had much time and he didn't especially like to talk. When he did, he focused on the clinical parts of the process. We were frustrated. One afternoon shortly after the surgery, I stopped Dr. Blue Eyes in the hallway. Standing a few doors down from Mom's room, we spoke in low voices. Short questions prompted short answers. I was tired and anxious. I recall the conversation going something like this:

"Where do you think this is headed?"

As he'd said before, the surgery had gone well. Chemo would be next. He'd be monitoring her closely.

"But . . . what should we expect?"

"Every patient is different," he said.

"I *understand* that," I responded, "but you must have some idea of what this is going to look like."

"You can't predict."

I didn't want him to predict, just to tell us what Mom was up against and how he felt it would play out, based on his experience and her condition.

I turned the question around.

"Look, if this were your mother, wouldn't you want to know? Wouldn't you be asking these same questions?"

The doctor took a breath and considered for a moment. He spoke slowly and deliberately.

"Typically, patients will go through cycles," he said. "Surgery and the first chemotherapy give her some breathing room."

"How much?" I asked.

"Usually eighteen months or so. But then the cancer can return."

"Then what?"

"We try another round of chemotherapy and see how that works. Generally, that knocks the cancer down for another six months or so.

"And?"

"We keep going. We find the drug that works best. Ideally, we manage the disease like other chronic illnesses." He said that the impact of the chemo often diminishes over time.

"How long can this go on?" I asked.

He hesitated. "The most common is about four years. But there are exceptions. It can go well. Some patients can live very long lives." We hoped Mom would be one of them.

That little Q&A with Dr. Blue Eyes still plays in my head. I had done some research and I knew generally what we were up against. But I could tell this was going to be even harder than we had anticipated. We needed the doctor's insight. We wanted to know what he knew. We also wanted to make clear that we were totally engaged and expected to be fully informed. This had to be a partnership and we were entitled to ask.

What's happening?
How do you know?
Have you seen this before?
What else aren't you telling us?
Would you say this to your mother?

It can be intimidating to question the expert. But effective advocacy requires tough questioning. Whether it's your mother or your business, your body or your roof, write out a list of questions and don't let up until every one of them is addressed. If the specialist you've chosen can't or won't answer your questions, see that as a red flag, a clear sign that you need to get a second (or third) opinion. Ask more until you're comfortable that you understand the problem and the pros and cons of each possible solution.

After the Diagnosis, the Strategy

Al Darby, Steve Miller, and Teresa Gardner lead very different lives, but they all use diagnostic inquiry to identify and solve problems. They question with open ears. They ask why the problem exists and where it comes from. They look for bad news. They ask about the past as well as the present. They work under pressure. They listen for detail, and they seek a cure.

That's how Teresa became well known. She was profiled on *60 Minutes*, the longest-running TV magazine show in America, with an audience of more than 10 million television watchers and millions more online. The story showed her driving her beat-up old Winnebago through Appalachia, asking her questions to treat her treasured "human train wrecks." It revealed the dimension of the problem and her commitment to address it. The attention was more than she bargained for, but speaking invitations and donations followed and Teresa finally got a new Winnebago Health Wagon.

Diagnostic questions identify a problem, a cause, and a response and take you to the next level:

> *Now what?*
> *What's the risk associated with the treatment?*
> *What should we be watching for?*

Steve Miller thinks CEOs should lie awake at night asking what's-gone-wrong questions so they can move on to the really big questions.

> *Are we in the right business?*
> *Are we looking forward?*
> *Do we fully envision the problems and opportunities ahead?*
> *Do we stand for the right values?*
> *Do we have a sustainable business model?*

Whether you are a Wall Street tycoon, a nurse practitioner in Appalachia or anything in between, only after you diagnose the situation can you move to the next level of inquiry, where you set your sights and ask about long-range challenges and opportunities in pursuit of an ambitious goal.

CHAPTER 3

THE GENERAL'S CHARGE
Strategic Questions

BILL AND MELINDA GATES didn't just wake up one morning and decide, over a bowl of organic oatmeal, to throw themselves and their money at the fight against malaria. They knew the terrible toll of the disease—symptoms that usually appear within two weeks of the mosquito bite: fever, chills, headache, and vomiting. They knew that, if not treated within twenty-four hours, the illness can become acute and kill. They'd seen the data: The disease was afflicting up to 300 million people a year. Most were pregnant women and children. Most were in Africa.

With their vast wealth and giant foundation, they were looking for philanthropic investments that could make the biggest difference for the most people. At a forum of more than 300 health and political leaders in 2007, Melinda Gates called for an all-out assault: "Advances in science and medicine, promising research, and the rising concern of people around the world represent a historic opportunity not just to treat malaria or to control it, but to chart a long-term course to eradicate it."

The call to eradicate malaria led to one of the most ambitious mobilizations of research and medicine in the world. Researchers and doctors made tremendous progress—in just a few years deaths came down 50 percent—but if the campaign actually eradicated the disease, it would save millions more lives and untold suffering. It would unlock immense potential in places where the disease is a debilitating curse on families, communities, and entire countries. Defeating malaria would be an epic human achievement. Like other ambitious undertakings, it requires huge investment, commitment, strategic alliances, massive time allotments, and boundless energy. But how did the Bill and Melinda Gates Foundation and others determine that an ambitious campaign against malaria was feasible and could succeed? What did they ask about objectives, resources, hurdles and challenges that made them come down on the side of an all-out assault? They posed big, strategic questions.

> *What is the extent of the problem?*
> *What will it take to succeed?*
> *Are we up to the challenge?*

In Chapter 2, I showed you how diagnostic questions help identify a particular problem that's defined by a unique set of symptoms or circumstances. Strategic questions ask about the bigger challenge and the long-term goal—about stakes, opportunities, costs, consequences, and alternatives—as you focus on the big picture. They help you set your sights, clarify objectives, and consider obstacles as you think about future benefits and consequences.

Set Your Sights

Perhaps you've been invited to join a startup venture. You like the people. They have a couple of years of funding. The business plan is exciting. There could be a big payoff. But the idea is untested and the competition is moving fast. You'll have to leave your corporate job, and there's no job security in the startup world.

Maybe your partner is lobbying for a move across the country to get out of the rat race and reboot your lives. The idea has appeal. But you're not sure what you will do out there, or how much of a real difference the move will make. Truth is, you're not loving life right now either, but this would be a quantum leap into the unknown. Will the change be worth the effort? And what about that paycheck you now get reliably every two weeks?

Your company is considering a major investment in a product that it believes will increase market share. You have to weigh in. Something is needed because the competition is eating your lunch and just launched a brilliant ad campaign that brought it a ton of buzz. Maybe the new product will make a difference, but it will require a huge investment, a lot of your time, and a big marketing push. It seems pretty cool, but there's no guarantee it will be the blockbuster you need.

These are all-in moves that come with a daunting list of pros and cons and plenty of unknowns. They call for fundamental changes and new ways of thinking. They require questions that look over the horizon.

"Strategy, by definition, is about making complex decisions under uncertainty, with substantive, long-term consequences," Freek Vermeulen, associate professor of strategy and entrepreneurship at the London Business School, wrote in the *Harvard Business Review* in September 2015. Vermeulen crafted an elegantly simple description of a word that almost everyone overuses and poorly understands. But by asking strategic questions, you can define and articulate your long-term goals. As you challenge your assumptions, you weigh the investment and risks involved. These are tough questions, built on a few overarching principles. Like an imaging satellite miles above the earth, strategic questions start wide and zoom in to see the landscape in detail.

Get the big picture. Define the challenge or opportunity. Ask why it matters. Articulate the goal. Does it reflect your values? Who else cares? What are others prepared to do? What does it look like from 60,000 feet?

Know what you're up against. Recognize that you have a worthy opponent, whether it's a person, place, or, in the Gates's case, a disease. Give it credit. It's the biggest obstacle that stands in your way. Ask what your opponent can dish out and what you're willing to take.

Define your plan. Determine the tactics that will help you achieve your strategic goal. What are the next steps and the steps down the road? Who does what? And how will you measure success along the way? Know that tactics may change even as your strategic interests remain constant.

Challenge yourself. Hold your plan or proposal up to the light and look for holes. Play out different scenarios. What haven't you thought of? What can go wrong? Can you explain and defend the strategy with facts, or is emotion driving you? Force yourself to stop and ask about options and alternatives.

Define success. Can you explain what success looks like? How will you know it when you achieve it? What will it take and at what cost?

A Strategic Approach

Before the Bill and Melinda Gates Foundation committed time and resources to the global fight against malaria, it posed a set of demanding questions to assess the dimension of the challenge. The foundation had published the "Strategy Lifecycle" as a sort of handbook of strategic questioning. The guide could serve as a template for just about any big decision, or campaign.

The Strategy Lifecycle posed a series of questions organized in three phases: Lookback and Scoping, Strategy Choice, and Execution Plan. "Look Back" and "Scoping" questions sought to learn from previous experiences and to define the history and dimensions of the issue.

> *What are the lessons from prior strategies and implications for our future work?*
> *What is the nature of the problem?*
> *What are the most promising ways to address the problem?*

Strategy Choice questions got specific, tied directly to the challenge and what was needed to accomplish the mission.

> *How do we think change will happen?*
> *What will we do and not do? Why? What are the trade-offs?*
> *What is the role of our partners?*
> *What are the financial requirements?*
> *How will we measure our results?*
> *What are the risks?*

The answers to these questions helped set the parameters of the undertaking, and they exposed the risks. The team then asked *how* and what it would take to achieve the defined goals.

> *What is the timing and sequencing of initiatives?*
> *What resources are needed?*

The foundation's strategic questions helped clarify decision-making and provide coherence to a campaign that pitted ambitious ideas against a formidable foe. The Gates Foundation launched its campaign and became a transformational leader in the fight against malaria. It spent billions of dollars to create new partnerships, launch massive public health campaigns, distribute insecticide-treated bed nets, and fund indoor spraying, more rapid diagnostic tests, more accessible treatments therapies, and a lot of research into improved medication. It helped turn the corner on malaria, especially in sub-Saharan Africa. The World Health Organization's *World Malaria Report 2014* estimated that malaria mortality rates had decreased by 47 percent globally and 54 percent in Africa since 2000. Researchers reported progress on a number of other fronts, including single-dose treatments and, possibly, a vaccine that would prevent the disease altogether. Optimists believe the disease can be eradicated by 2030.

A General's Command

Strategic questions deepen understanding and clarify objectives. By asking more, you set benchmarks and assess risk. You examine opportunities and expose vulnerabilities. You become a better thinker and a smarter leader. You avoid the constraints of near-term distractions and stay focused on the essential, long-term goals. To dig into strategic questioning with someone who has done it for a living, I crossed the river to Virginia to pay a visit to General Colin Powell.

Headquartered in a nondescript office building just off the George Washington Parkway, the general still had the bearing of a military man. Taut and trim, he looked much younger than his seventy-odd years. He greeted me warmly with a big smile and an outstretched hand. I wanted to learn about his version of the strategy lifecycle—how he had brought military discipline together with intellectual curiosity to clarify the mission and set strategy at a time of war when the stakes couldn't be higher. I wanted to know how this retired four-star general had used questions to define and execute a mission. I wanted him to explain success. And failure.

I had first met Colin Powell when we were both much younger. He was a rising star and had just been named President Ronald Reagan's national security adviser. He took the job in the wake of the Iran-Contra scandal, an unmitigated disaster that threatened the Reagan presidency. Lieutenant Colonel Oliver North and others had hatched a secret scheme, run out of the White House, to sell arms to Iran in exchange for American hostages and funnel the profits to anticommunist guerrillas in Nicaragua. The convoluted mission violated U.S. laws as well as the president's solemn pledge never to negotiate with terrorists. It was a mess.

I was a young White House correspondent with an untested news organization called CNN. I became consumed by the story and the deepening scandal—following every move of the independent counsel, months of congressional hearings, and leaks from sources trying to influence public opinion and the investigation itself. The scandal ruined careers and tarnished the Reagan presidency. Several senior officials resigned or were thrown overboard.

Reluctantly, President Reagan finally acknowledged, "Mistakes were made."

Powell was a calming influence. He was brought in to help repair the severely damaged ship of state. He stayed above the chaos and proved adept at managing it. I remember his first White House briefings. His unflappable demeanor and disarming ability to pivot from tough guy to humorous answer man established him as a confident and credible power player. His direct, sometimes playful relationship with the media made him a go-to person for a comment or quote.

Everybody, it seemed, respected Colin Powell. He would serve three other presidents—George H. W. Bush, Bill Clinton, and George W. Bush, breaking barriers as the first African American in some of the most influential roles in the U.S. government.

When I visited his office all these years later, Powell's roles in government service long finished, I was struck by its modesty. The picture windows looked out on the GW Parkway, not on the grand avenues or monuments of Washington that so many crave in order to assert their place in history. Inside, there was no wall of fame heavy with pictures of Powell in uniform or alongside world leaders, no reminders of famous battles or personal glory that are so common in the offices of "formers" across this power town. The most prominent object was parked next to Powell's desk: a bright red Radio Flyer wagon, the symbol of America's Promise, the youth organization Powell founded nearly twenty years before.

Colin Powell was a key player in America's two wars against Iraq. In the first, he was chairman of the Joint Chiefs of Staff, the principal military adviser to President George H. W. Bush. In the second, he was secretary of state, the top diplomat in the cabinet serving President George W. Bush. Powell was not the principal architect or the leading voice in either war—there were many other forces and personalities at work in both—but he played significant roles. The questions he asked—and did not ask—stand as examples of how strategic questioning can shape decision-making at a time of crisis.

Powell explained that his approach to strategic questioning was honed through his military training. During his student days in the Reserve Officers' Training Corps (ROTC) he learned to start with a rapid and accurate "estimate of the situation," so he would know what he was up against. Suppose there's a hill to be taken, Powell said, the first thing the young infantry officer or the old corps commander needs to do is ask:

What's up there?
How many enemy?
What's the weather going to be like?
How much time do I have?
How much equipment?
How much food?
What's my ammunition supply rate?
What's the enemy doing?
How dug in is he?
What's his ability to reinforce?

Once you assess your opponent's ability, Powell explained, you devise a plan that includes tactics and timelines. Your success in taking that hill will depend on having asked the right questions so you have the most accurate "estimate of the situation" possible.

As Powell rose in the ranks, his world expanded well beyond the hill to be taken. Increasingly, he had to think about winning the war, not just the battle. He developed *strategic questions* designed to look at the big picture, articulate goals, and challenge his thinking and that of his commanders. Powell's strategic questions asked decision-makers to peel back groupthink and conventional wisdom, recognizing Vermeulen's definition of strategy and the stakes of "complex decisions under uncertainty, with substantive, long-term consequences."

Eight Yeses

Powell's big test as a military leader came after Iraq invaded Kuwait in August 1990. Saddam Hussein's invasion was a sledge-hammered move in a fragile region, a dictator's crass grab for power and territory. By occupying Kuwait, he also posed a threat to Saudi Arabia, America's oil-rich ally. President George H. W. Bush declared that the aggression "will not stand." The president wanted a recommendation. The first questions, Powell explained to me, sought to define the mission.

"The early argument was what do you want to do? Do you just want to protect Saudi Arabia so that the Iraqis can't move south? Or do you want to kick the Iraqis out of Kuwait? And is there anything else you want to do? You want to go to Baghdad? And we needed to get those questions answered . . . before we made a plan," he said.

There was no appetite to go to Baghdad, least of all from Powell. He told the president that if the United States pursued Saddam and marched into Baghdad, "You are going to be the proud owner of 25 million people. You will own all their hopes, aspirations, and problems. You'll own it all."

So the Pentagon went to work, putting together a military campaign, Operation Desert Storm, to liberate Kuwait. Planners considered Iraq's military capacity, topography, roads, ports, waterways, weather, and the location of civilian populations. They looked at American capabilities and the contributions allied forces could make. Before proposing to the president the deployment of half a million American troops to push Saddam Hussein back across the desert, however, Powell asked his strategic questions to see what they would reveal through the long lens of diplomacy, politics, and war. He wanted to know about goals, resources, consequences, rationale, and risk. Having experienced Vietnam, he asked whether the American public would stand by a war in Iraq if it got costly and difficult.

Powell posed eight strategic questions looking at the big picture, challenging assumptions, and defining success. Only if the answers to all were positive, he believed, could the president confidently launch a full-scale invasion to liberate Kuwait.

Is a vital national security interest threatened?

Is the action supported by the American people?

Do we have genuine, broad international support?

Have the risks and costs been fully and frankly analyzed?

Have all other nonviolent policy means been fully exhausted?

Have the consequences of our action been fully considered?

Do we have a clear, attainable objective?

Is there a plausible exit strategy to avoid endless entanglement?

The answers were all compelling and affirmative. The big-picture questions made clear the threats to national and global security. Iraq had broken international law and was sowing instability in a region that provided much of the world's oil and access to some of its most important shipping lanes. Public support appeared solid, with the U.S. Congress voting for military force and three in four of Americans supporting it, according to a Gallup survey at the time. The international community was on board, too. UN Resolution 678 authorized all necessary means to push Iraq out of Kuwait. Several countries in the region, even some that were normally hostile to Washington, signed on as active coalition partners.

Powell's challenge questions drew definitive responses as well. Intelligence from U.S. sources, as well as from Iraq's neighbors and America's closest allies, painted a consistent picture of Saddam's intentions and capabilities. The option of diplomacy had been tried through intermediaries, the United Nations, and direct talks with the Iraqi foreign minister. America had consulted every country in the region, along with more than two dozen coalition partners. Military and political leaders had considered every contingency they could think of, down to the frightening scenario that Iraq might sabotage its oil fields, which ultimately, it did.

Finally, Powell's questions intended to define success produced clear answers and finite, achievable goals with a realistic exit strategy. The result was a mission—Operation Desert Storm—designed to push Saddam out of Kuwait and force him to comply with international law and UN resolutions. This would not be an open-ended occupation or an exercise in nation building.

The war began with a punishing barrage from the air. American and coalition bombing pounded Iraq's air defenses, military installations, and government headquarters, which were quickly destroyed. By the time U.S. and coalition forces rolled into Kuwait on the ground, Iraqi forces were on the run. Though Saddam hung on to power, the mission had been a success.

The ground war lasted just 100 hours. Colin Powell's star was never higher.

Failure Is an Option

When a leader fails to know where he is going, refuses to listen to what he doesn't want to hear, or relies on faulty information, bad things happen. If nobody asks or answers challenging questions, flawed thinking may go unnoticed or unaddressed. Colin Powell experienced the dark side of decision-making when he and others didn't ask enough tough questions leading up to the *second* Iraq war.

In the aftermath of the terror attacks of September 11, 2001, Powell, then Secretary of State, was surrounded by hard-liners, led by Vice President Dick Cheney, Defense Secretary Donald Rumsfeld, and several influential senior policy makers. Cheney and the others argued for a muscular American military response. After Afghanistan, home to Al Qaeda, they viewed Iraq as a logical target. They accused Iraq of harboring weapons of mass destruction, in direct violation of commitments to destroy them made after the first Gulf War.

Still reeling from the 9/11 attacks on New York's World Trade Towers and the Pentagon in Washington, D.C., the public strongly supported this administration's plans for military action against Iraq. The administration assured the world that the intelligence was credible and the Iraqi threat with respect to weapons of mass destruction was real. But behind the scenes, the really tough strategic questions that should have been asked were unwelcome.

> *Have the risks and costs been fully and frankly analyzed?*
> *Have the consequences of our action been fully considered?*
> *Do we have a clear and attainable objective?*

The questions Powell posed before the first Iraq war, more relevant than ever, were glossed over or not pursued. Powell himself contributed to the drumbeat to war in a dramatic 2003 appearance before the United Nations.

"Leaving Saddam Hussein in possession of weapons of mass destruction for a few more months or years is not an option," Powell declared. "Not in a post–September 11 world."

As experience would later show, however, Saddam didn't have weapons of mass destruction. The intelligence was wrong. The administration hadn't asked the right questions of the right people. I asked Powell about the price he and America paid for that failure. For the first time in our otherwise friendly conversation, he bristled. The information he got was bad, he said. It had gone to Congress four months before he went to the UN. Congress had seen the formal National Intelligence Estimate, the comprehensive report prepared by the CIA, and reached the same conclusions. Influential senators on both sides of the aisle including John Kerry, Hillary Clinton, John McCain, and Jay Rockefeller, the chairman of the Senate Intelligence Committee, all lined up behind the report. The president cited it in his State of the Union speech. Vice President Dick Cheney went on national television with it. Condoleezza Rice, the national security adviser, referred to it when she told CNN that Saddam was closer to a nuclear device than anybody thought. "We know that he has the infrastructure, nuclear scientists to make a nuclear weapon," Rice had said, adding ominously, "but we don't want the smoking gun to be a mushroom cloud."

"They all said this is solid stuff and believed it," Powell told me.

They were all wrong.

Particularly egregious was the assertion that the Iraqis had biological weapons laboratories that they could move around and hide from weapons inspectors and spy satellites. It was Exhibit A for the CIA. But it was based on a single source, an Iraqi defector code-named Curveball. He'd told his story to German intelligence. American agents never interrogated him. Only after the invasion did we learn that Curveball had lied.

Why didn't anyone realize Curveball's story was full of holes? What questions should have been asked, and by whom? Why didn't alarm bells ring when officials realized Curveball had not been interrogated by American agents? More than ten years after the fact, Powell was still steaming mad.

"The friggin' director of the CIA should have asked! He should have asked his people, 'What do we really know about this? . . . Where did this come from? Is it multiple-sourced?'"

As secretary of state, Powell didn't push back hard enough. The power players—the vice president, the secretary of defense, and others—drove the decisions. They didn't ask the right questions either. The U.S. mission in Iraq turned into a costly open-ended commitment riddled with unintended consequences and terrible casualties, resulting in an ugly and inconclusive outcome.

"Yes, a blot, a failure will always be attached to me and my UN presentation," Powell wrote in his book, *It Worked for Me*. "I am mad mostly at myself for not having smelled the problem. My instincts failed me."

In his office, far from the cameras and the lights, the retired general and former secretary of state seemed subdued and regretful that his long and distinguished life of service to the United States, his record of breaking barriers and standing for integrity and honor, had been sullied by a mission that he and others did not submit to the kind of scrutiny and strategic questioning it deserved. His UN appearance and his insistence that Saddam Hussein represented a clear and present danger still pained him.

"I'm the one left holding the bag with respect to all this crap and it's in my obituary," he said to me. "And so be it."

Washington is a town of towering purpose but also towering egos. It is a place where people assess you by your connections and your access to power, where you are only as useful as your last job title and the network you bring with you. Taking responsibility for failure and screw-ups is not a common trait. It's too easy to accuse someone else, duck the tough questions, or change the subject. Powell didn't do that. He acknowledged when an operation had gone wrong and he took responsibility where it mattered. He should have been a louder voice and insisted that difficult but strategic questions got asked along the way. Whether anyone would have listened to him is another matter. But he knows he should have tried. That's a lesson from him and for the rest of us.

Getting Personal

In the mid-1990's, when his star dominated the political horizon, Powell considered a run for the White House. The pressure from supporters was intense. The calling seemed clear. Powell's first book, *My American Journey*, was a bestseller. America's victory against Saddam Hussein in the first Gulf War, and the four stars on Powell's shoulders, made him a hero. His story was inspiring and he enjoyed unparalleled stature and authority. He looked like a modern-day Eisenhower, a leader who could bring precision and discipline to Washington, along with star quality and diversity to the Republican Party. The very hint of a Powell presidential bid drove cable news shows and op-ed columns into a frenzy. I was the anchor of a daily show on CNN at the time, and we could barely keep the pundits and politicians away from the microphone. Everybody wanted to weigh in. It was TV heaven, but the spectacle was short-lived.

Powell asked his strategic questions, this time on a much more personal level.

One, do I have an obligation?
Two, do I really want to do it?
Three, do I have the passion to do it?
Four, do I have the organizational ability to do it?
Five, am I going to enjoy campaigning or will I be good at it?
Six, what is my family's view of this?

Could he answer each question in the affirmative? No, he didn't have the passion. And no, his family was not on board—especially his wife, Alma, who had suffered bouts of depression over the years. To submit her to the unending ordeal of a campaign and the intense and public pressures of the White House should he win were beyond what he could reasonably ask. The world would never see a Powell candidacy.

Instead, Powell would serve as secretary of state in one of the most wrenching periods in American history. There would be speeches and books and boards. And when it was all over, he would have his regrets but he'd still have his integrity, service to country, and his general's bearing. And he would proudly display that little red wagon in his office, dedicated to America's Promise.

Challenge Yourself

Strategic questions are vital company at any major crossroads, professional or personal. They are deceptively simple questions that illuminate complex decisions characterized by great risk or uncertainty. They are healthy questions that call for answers about purpose and the big picture.

You may decide, like Colin Powell, that the answers need to be unanimous and affirmative. Or you may be comfortable with a more ambiguous response. After all, some of the best ideas and strategies have been built on hunches or whims. But strategic questions prompt you to examine the terrain broadly, to estimate the situation from which you can proceed with a better sense of capability and destination. Whether you are considering a major business move or a big investment of your own time and resources, thinking about the long-term consequences and goals—asking why, where, and how—will help you to better clarify the stakes and the prospects. At a major crossroad, pose a variation of these questions to yourself or the group:

Does this course of action advance my interests?
Is there a calling, a bigger purpose?
Does it feel right—is it important, consistent with my values?
Do I have the passion to do this and stick with it?
Can I define "success"?
Do I have the tools to achieve it?
Have I calculated costs and benefits, risks, rewards, and alternatives?
What are the consequences for my emotional, intellectual, and spiritual well-being?

Would the people closest to me think this is a good idea?
*If this ended up in my biography (or obituary), would I be proud to
see it there?*

As the Bill and Melinda Gates Foundation considered its campaign
against malaria, the answers to their strategic questions pointed to a
need, a capability, and a plan that justified a massive global campaign.
They have since worked with doctors and scientists, governments and
nongovernmental organizations (NGOs), community organizers and
ordinary citizens to make significant progress against a deadly disease.
Big and bold and ambitious, their all-in strategy produced results that
justified the cost and the risk. Their strategy, well considered and exe-
cuted, attacked the right problem and was built on the right questions.

CHAPTER 4

FROM THE INSIDE OUT
Empathy Questions

I SAT DOWN WITH four young moms. They arranged themselves in a semicircle so we could all see each other. They were polite, soft-spoken, nicely dressed, and anxious to talk about themselves and their children. A diverse group—black and white and Hispanic—all of them were single moms and receiving some form of public assistance.

I was there to do a story for CNN on welfare reform from the perspective of those receiving the benefits—the people we don't hear from very often, the people we talk *about*, but seldom *with*. I wanted to hear about their lives and explore with them how the proposed changes would affect them. The welfare reform law, known formally as the Personal Responsibility and Work Opportunity Act of 1996, sparked heated debate and controversy. It placed time limits on welfare benefits, required recipients to find work, tightened child support enforcement, and tried to discourage out-of-wedlock births by limiting benefits for young single parents. I had heard an endless parade of politicians and experts sound off on the issue. But I was curious: how did these proposed changes look through the eyes of the people who would be directly affected by them? So I asked.

What difference will this new law make?
What kind of job do you want?
How will a job help you make ends meet?

They all said a job would improve their lives and their finances. A job would give them self-respect and a steady income would help them be better parents. But they still needed to take care of their children. They still needed healthcare. They worried about whether their paycheck would be enough to feed the whole family. They wanted to work, but they had valid concerns—and a lot of questions.

As the conversation unfolded and I learned about their lives, I discovered a much more complicated reality than I had imagined. Three of the women had struggled with alcohol or drug issues. One had six kids, including a son who was born with a heart defect and needed frequent medical care. None of these women had gone to college. One said she could barely read.

One of the moms told me about a job interview she had coming up at a local hospital. She was excited and preparing for it. What was the job? I asked. Working in reception or something, she replied. What did it pay? Minimum wage, she thought. How would she afford childcare on minimum wage? Would she have healthcare? How would she get to and from work? She had no idea.

As the conversation unfolded, I realized that the real story here was how much we didn't know and couldn't imagine. These women lived fractured and difficult lives, filled with struggle and pain, sometimes of their own doing. I did my best to capture the conversation, but I wished the public could have been there, asking these questions and hearing the answers for themselves, because these women—despite every expectation and stereotype—were inspiring in their determination. You got a different perspective if you asked:

What do you see when you wake up each day?
What are you feeling, fearing, and thinking?
What do you want for your children?

The questions that have always interested me the most are the ones that explore people as three-dimensional beings, each with a unique and layered story. They are questions that mine the most complex human elements, revealing depth of soul and experience. They are questions that foster understanding of someone you don't know or who is very different from you.

These questions—*empathy questions*—explore what makes people tick, think, fear, and feel. They focus unselfishly and spring from genuine interest. The simple act of asking, of listening without comment or judgment and letting a silence linger or a free-form thought coalesce, invites a person to reflect or think out loud. It might even prompt a revelation.

Empathetic questioning helps you connect with a friend who is going through a divorce, a family member who has cancer, a teenager who is struggling with grades and social hierarchy, or a welfare mom. Use this line of inquiry when a colleague needs to talk through an argument at home or politics at the office, or when you want to reach out to someone who comes from a different place, background, or perspective.

In this chapter, I explore empathetic questioning through the prism of example and from the perspective of those who've studied it and done it for a living. They know how to use questions to enhance trust, reinforce relationships, and improve our understanding of ourselves. This form of questioning pays off in a number of ways. Research shows empathetic bosses inspire more productive workers. Empathetic doctors are more effective. A variety of studies has linked empathy to better health outcomes and lower stress levels. A study published in the *Journal of the Association of American Medical Colleges* in 2011 found that diabetes patients did a better job regulating their blood sugar when being treated by empathetic doctors. Other studies have found that cancer patients had greater trust in doctors who responded to them empathetically and reported less depression and better quality of life.

Using questions to establish empathetic relationships involves seeing and asking from another perspective. Ask to:

Try new shoes. Empathy involves taking the perspective of another person. What is he thinking? How is he feeling? If you switched places and stood in his shoes, what would you see?

Leave running room. Start with big broad questions to get people talking. Invite them to engage on ground where they're most comfortable and most familiar.

Listen beyond words. The deeper you go, the more you need to listen for cues and tone and mood. Pauses and hesitation have meaning, too. So do body language, facial expressions, and eye contact.

Establish intimate distance. Convey compassion and interest. But maintain enough distance and detachment so you don't judge and can offer objective questions or advice.

The Good Professor

Helen Riess is a clinical professor of psychiatry at Harvard Medical School. She studies empathy and teaches doctors how to incorporate it into their work with patients. I got to know her through the Middlebury College board we both served on. From the moment I met her I was struck by her instinctive ability to listen intently and to represent diverse viewpoints with depth and sensitivity when she spoke at our meetings. When she mentioned student life, for example, she conveyed a special awareness of the pressures college students face, engulfed by technology, plugged in to always-on texting, dealing with mountains of debt and uncertain employment in a hypercompetitive global economy.

As I learned about her background and her interests, I discovered that Helen was an expert on empathy. She researched it, taught it, wrote about it, practiced it, and coached it. I wanted to know how she thought the rest of us could better leverage empathy through the questions we asked, so I went to see her in Boston.

We met at a restaurant near her office, a few blocks from Massachusetts General Hospital, where she was director of the Empathy and Relational Science Program. Helen practiced what she taught: As we sat and talked, she leaned in, locked eyes, and maintained a relaxed and comfortable demeanor. She listened intently—no smartphone intrusions here—and did not break her gaze, barely looking down at her lunch.

Helen described empathy to me as "the ability to listen and take another person's perspective." It empowers you not just to understand the other person but also to imagine you are the other person, she said. "Perspective taking" is a way of asking people to assume another person's viewpoints, emotions, behaviors, and thoughts—to see through their lens in order to understand their point of view.

"This is where imagination and curiosity come in," Helen told me. "This is the intentional act of moving yourself out of your shoes and into the shoes of the other person." Empathy is not asking "What would it be like for me?" she explained, but "I wonder what it would be like for him?" Her empathetic questions reflect that "perspective taking."

What's it like to experience what that person's going through?
What are other people feeling?
Scared? Jubilant? Vulnerable?
What is it like for them to be who they are?

Helen works with doctors. She tells them to start with a broad question to establish an empathetic relationship. It is the simplest of questions, yet if it is meant sincerely, it can both solicit useful information and convey genuine concern.

How are you doing today?

But Helen tells her doctors that they have to do more than just ask. They have to listen, closely and sincerely. They have to hear more than words. They must listen to voice tone and inflection and watch for reactions and body language. She coaches them to maintain eye contact and scan the other person's face to see if they seem relaxed, anxious, frightened, or stressed. If they hear strong emotion, they should respond to it directly and ask compassionately.

What are you most concerned about?

Helen urges her doctors to stay off the computer when a patient is talking, interrupt as little as possible, and stay calm and respond reassuringly when a patient expresses emotion or fear. Tune into their words and cues. Focus intentionally and supportively to establish empathy and convey it.

Helen believes it is the questioner's responsibility to take in fully what the patient is communicating. This affects outcomes; patients who don't experience empathy are less likely to trust their doctors and they're less likely to adhere to the treatments that are recommended. They are much less satisfied. Helen's research has corroborated these findings.

"We did a study, a systematic review and a meta-analysis . . . that showed that low empathy and communication in patient-doctor relationships actually leads to worse health outcomes, statistically significant worse obesity, hypertension, asthma, osteoarthritis pain. These are hard health outcomes that are affected when there's a poor connection." Helen explained that one of her graduate students found that doctors' stress levels also improved when they had empathetic relationships with their patients.

Empathy ratifies our humanity. Walt Whitman captured its essence when he wrote, "I do not ask the wounded person how he feels. I myself become the wounded person." The best questioners take Whitman's words to heart.

Which is why I went to talk to Terry Gross.

The Empathetic Interviewer

WHYY radio is located in downtown Philadelphia. The station offers twenty-four hours of programming, but one voice is known to millions.

As host of NPR's *Fresh Air* program, Terry Gross has interviewed thousands of people. Her questions have a signature quality, clear and curious, understated, and often deeply empathetic. Her questions draw out her guests, allowing her to get inside their heads and connect. Some 4.5 million people every week hear her show on more than 400 radio stations and countless podcasts across America. Terry has developed a special style and voice for interviewing creative types: authors and artists, actors and musicians, thinkers and theoreticians.

Rail thin and barely five feet tall, Terry's physical presence belies her stature as one of the most gifted interviewers in broadcasting. She greeted me in the lobby and took me to one of the station's main studios. Having started my career in radio, I felt at home in this dusky, unadorned box of a room dominated only by a desk, a few chairs, and a couple of microphones on extension arms that could swivel as needed. We settled in for our conversation, a couple of believers in the magic of radio and the revealed secrets of interview. There is something intensely private about radio. There are no distractions, no bright lights or cameras that will catch you off guard. People are more relaxed in radio. The listener paints his or her own picture of the faces that go with the voices.

Interviewing on the radio was an unexpected career for Terry. As a girl, she was shy, quiet, and not inclined to share anything personal, especially information about herself or her family. Her grandparents were Russian and Polish Jews who escaped to America. They did not discuss the dark times or details about family members. They felt that "there were a lot of things historically you just don't tell people."

Terry started to find her voice when she got a job in radio in Buffalo, New York. The station featured programming for women. For her job application, Terry had to write sample questions for one of the station's hosts, a feminist lawyer, who was doing a show about women and divorce. Terry was going through a divorce herself, so the questions came quickly and easily. She got the job.

Because it was the 1970s, a college campus, and blissfully egalitarian public radio, everyone got a shot. Terry started doing some hosting. She loved it and the job loved her. She recalled a show featuring the feminist take on women's undergarments. Did they objectify women? She did another discussing women as sexualized victims in popular culture, with a sadomasochistic consideration of Dracula as a public sex offender. The old vampire "was so S&M," Terry told me with a mischievous grin.

Two years later she moved to Philadelphia and WHYY. The station has been her home ever since.

Terry's first rule of interviewing is "know your guest." Find the most interesting parts of their lives and stories. Read, listen, and watch them. "The more you know about someone, and the more you genuinely care about them, the more likely they are to trust you with their story," she explained. Put yourself in their place. Do some perspective taking. "The more they trust you with their story, the more they'll open up. The more they open up, the more fascinating they will be."

Terry asks her guests about their experiences and ideas. She wants to know their origins and what inspires them. She asks about the things that shape people, especially creative people like artists, musicians, actors, authors, thinkers. She finds that breaking her questions into small pieces is an effective way to generate specific answers that connect to stories and prompt reflection.

"You can ask questions about their childhood and find out, were they sick, were they well?" she says. "Just all those things that create who you are."

> *Were they outgoing or inhibited?*
> *Were they good in school, and did they like school?*
> *What were their parents like, and where were they from?*
> *How were they parented?*
> *Did they like to read?*
> *Did they go to the movies?*
> *What were the first records they bought?*

In a powerful interview with comedian Tracy Morgan, Terry dug down to the roots of a troubled adolescence that nurtured Morgan's latent creativity. Notice how she framed her questions without judgment but without hesitation.

GROSS: *So I just wanted to get back to your childhood a little bit. When your father died of AIDS when you were in high school, you dropped out of high school, and you needed money. So you say you started selling marijuana and then eventually started selling crack.*

MORGAN: *Yeah.*

GROSS: *But—so I'm wondering. Did you take Al Pacino's advice from* Scarface—*don't get high on your own supply?*

MORGAN: *No, I never did drugs. My drug of choice was beer, was liquor. As far as narcotics, no. I would smoke weed and drink beer like any other—like Michael Phelps do that. But I never did no narcotics—never. My father had died from that. So I already knew better. You know, I'm a very smart person. I was able to see that. As a child, I was able to know that I wanted a better life.*

GROSS: *You say that it was helpful to you as a comic to sell crack because of all the characters that you met. What do you mean?*

MORGAN: *Well, it wasn't helpful for me to sell crack, especially to my old community, and it still bothers me today, but it's something that I did. It was survival. Now I'm living. Now I don't have to do any of that stuff. I'm a grown man now, but when I did, I wasn't good at it. So I had my fledging attempt at being a drug dealer.*

GROSS: *So, tell me really, how did you feel when you were selling crack, knowing that you were selling a drug that destroys lives?*

MORGAN: *I was a kid. I had no fear. I was crazy, and when you don't have fear, you're crazy.*

Terry's questions penetrate gently but insistently. She is interested in creative tension, setback, and adversity, but she does not try to embarrass or trip up her guests. Her voice is warm and her listening accommodates the ranges of emotion she encounters.

"I'm not looking to shame somebody. I'm not looking to have them say anything that's going to keep them awake at night, regretting that they said it. I'm not looking to have them say something that's going to end up with their mother or their child or their best friend hating them for saying it."

Terry Gross prefers to let her guests take the lead when questions get personal and the emotions get rough: "I don't just sit down and ask people about their sexual orientation or their religion or their fear of death, unless it comes up organically in some way through their work or through something that they said."

That's where empathy plays a vital role. "I try to imagine what is it like to be that person," Terry explains. "What might they have been feeling when they did this or experienced this? And is there anything like that in my life, not because I want to talk with them about my life, but because I want to be able to understand it in a way that might make sense to me."

When Terry interviewed renowned author Maurice Sendak, her empathetic questioning produced a remarkable moment.

Sendak, the beloved children's author of *Where the Wild Things Are* and other books, was a famously complex character. He could translate dark reality into a playful children's adventure. An avowed atheist, he was introspective and deeply creative. He came out as gay late in life. In September 2011, as the New England fall was setting in, Sendak spoke with Terry by phone. He was eighty-three and in failing health. His partner was gone, and loneliness was his companion. But Sendak had just published *Bumble-Ardy*, a book about a pig who, on his ninth birthday, throws himself his first birthday party. The story is a fable about growing up and staying young, about celebration and convention, about love and forgiveness. Terry had interviewed Sendak many times before. They'd known one another for years. He trusted her. You can hear the affection in her voice.

She congratulates him on the book and asks simply:

How have you been?

Sendak sounds fatigued and resigned.

"It's been a rough time," he admits. He's gotten "quite old." He is still working but it doesn't matter if he ever publishes again. What time he has left is "for me and me alone." Sendak speaks about the death of his publisher and his publisher's wife. "My tears flow," he says. "I am having to deal with that and it's very, very hard."

There can be art in a question. Terry's next one paints with a deft stroke. Having heard Sendak's loneliness, feeling his mortality, she asks:

Are you at the point where you feel like you've outlived a lot of people who you loved?

"Yes. Of course," he answers. "And since I don't believe in another world, in another life, that this is it. And when they die they are out of my life. They're gone forever. Blank. Blank. Blank."

Terry acknowledges the thought: "Having friends die tests our faith." She knows Sendak does not believe in God and rejects religion. Still, she wonders whether he feels any spirituality as he considers his own death.

Is your atheism staying strong?

"Yes. I'm not unhappy about becoming old," he says. "I'm not unhappy about what must be. It makes me cry only when I see my friends go before me and life is emptied." He reflects on the hundred-year-old maple trees just outside his window. "I can see how beautiful they are. I can take time to see how beautiful they are. It is a blessing to get old."

As Terry thanks Sendak, thinking she is bringing the interview to a close, the conversation takes its most interesting turn. She hears more than his words. She picks up on his tone of voice, the way he paces his thoughts. She hovers on the moment.

GROSS: *Well, I'm really glad we got the chance to speak because when I heard you had a book coming out I thought what a good excuse . . . to call up Maurice Sendak and have a chat.*

SENDAK: *Yes, that's what we always do, isn't it?*

GROSS: *Yeah. It is.*

SENDAK: *That's what we've always done.*

GROSS: *It is.*

SENDAK: *Thank God we're still around to do it.*

GROSS: *Yes.*

SENDAK: *And almost certainly, I'll go before you go, so I won't have to miss you.*

GROSS: *Oh, God what a . . .*

SENDAK: *And I don't know whether I'll do another book or not. I might. It doesn't matter. I'm a happy old man. But I will cry my way all the way to the grave.*

GROSS: *Well, I'm so glad you have a new book. I'm really glad we had a chance to talk.*

SENDAK: *I am too.*

GROSS: *And I wish you all good things.*

SENDAK: *I wish you all good things. Live your life, live your life, live your life.*

Nearly poetic, Sendak spoke from his most solitary place, staring directly at the mortality that we are all destined to confront. Terry told me it was one of the most emotional interviews she has ever done.

"What struck me about him in that interview is that he opened the door without me even knocking, to talk about the things that I was uncomfortable even asking my parents about when I knew they were dying." Terry picked up on Sendak's cues. She followed him through his thought process. She asked gently. Perhaps without even realizing it, she stood in Sendak's shoes—alone, vulnerable, and exposed. She asked about hard things and conveyed her willingness to hear whatever came back. Then, she asked for more.

"That's the thing about interviewing," Terry explained, "You're there for the special thing, which is to dig deep and get to the essence of what it means to be you."

Whether you're a radio host, or a friend, a concerned parent, or a trusted colleague, empathetic questions can lead to discovery and surprise. They help you dig deep and do a little perspective-taking. They can also be achingly difficult because they may visit some intensely private places. Conversations that build on empathetic questioning require patient, skilled, and focused listening. Terry listens for the revealed moment, where an inner thought, emotion, or expression of the human condition unfurls. She listens for reflection, acknowledgement, or a telltale pause. She listens for illuminating stories that haven't been finished or heard before.

She creates what I call *intimate distance*. The intimacy is expressed through her evident interest in her guest. It is authenticated by her questions, which embrace human complexity and frailty. She maintains distance by sitting back, withholding judgment, letting silence linger, and retaining an outsider's eye. Intimate distance allows Terry to engage emotion without getting trapped by it or drawn in so that she forfeits her observer status.

Maurice Sendak died eight months after his interview with Terry Gross.

He published one more book after *Bumble-Ardy*. But it is the words from his most famous book, *Where the Wild Things Are*, that resonate and connect to Sendak's own journey through life.

I am holding the book now, tattered and worn, the binding barely holding the pages in place. I read this book so many times to my children when they were young that when I close my eyes I can feel those little people next to me, nestled with their innocence and wonderment against my younger self. I see the journey now, having completed so much of it.

Where the Wild Things Are tells the story of Max, the book's adventurous boy traveler, who put on his wolf suit, made mischief, and sailed away to rumble with the wild things. And when he decided it was time to go home, Max "sailed back over a year and in and out of weeks and through a day and into the night of his very own room where he found his supper waiting for him . . . and it was still hot."

It is that sense of place and that rhythm of the journey that Sendak was relaying to Terry Gross. What kid doesn't stand in Max's shoes and imagine—and empathize?

Therapeutic Inquiry

You don't need a degree to be a disciplined listener and an empathetic questioner. You just need to know who you are talking to and be able to imagine what the world looks like through their eyes. Terry explains that it's like mining what's beneath the surface.

"When I'm interviewing somebody," she says, "I'm drawing on the self-knowledge they already have. I'm not presuming to be a therapist and lead them to questions that will enable them to reach self-knowledge that they don't already have."

Terry is right to recognize that, however adept her questioning, traveling to the depths where the psyche holds its secrets, insecurities, repressed memories, and Freudian trappings is not what she's paid to do. That's someone else's job. Which is why I decided to see a therapist, someone trained to go to those places—carefully and over time, an empathetic questioner by definition.

I met Betty Pristera at the airport in Raleigh-Durham, North Carolina. She pulled up in her little Honda Civic, a fitting vehicle for this compact spring of a woman, who, I soon learned, was also a competitive ballroom dancer. She bounded out of the car to greet me.

"Welcome to Raleigh-Durham," she said with a beaming smile, "How *are* you?" She shook my hand, directed me to the passenger seat and began asking about my life before we were out of the airport. We headed to a nearby restaurant for a late breakfast, where we were waist-deep in conversation before the eggs hit the table.

A friend had introduced me to Betty after I'd mentioned to him that I wanted to explore how therapists use empathetic questioning to help people discover and heal. My friend had been through a rough time, and Betty helped him through it. He said she had listened and guided and *empathized*. She didn't judge. She drew him out and asked him to explore his life and his experiences in profoundly reflective ways. She helped him discover secrets he kept from himself so he could reconnect and get his life back on track. She maintained intimate distance.

I wanted to know how the rest of us could apply these techniques in our own questioning. What could we learn from this empathetic therapist to become more effective questioners?

Betty came from a large Italian family. She grew up in New Jersey. Her father was a chemist, her mom a housewife. She was nurtured on the traditions, flavors, and smells of southern Italy. There was always food and family in the house. And music. Everyone played something. Her father and brothers played the violin, her mother and sister played the piano. Several family members sang. Betty learned piano early. She was performing by the time she was nine. There was talk that she should go to Juilliard and make music her career. But she was drawn to people.

When Betty was eleven, she watched her grandfather die. Her mother maintained a bedside vigil, and Betty was nearby. The young girl witnessed her mother's "heart and courage" as she bore the pain of the dying man. Betty took the experience as a calling and became a hospital volunteer. Ultimately, she went to nursing school, earned a master's degree in social work, and studied marriage and family therapy. Her first job was at an adult day program at the Eastern Pennsylvania Psychiatric Institute, where she led group therapy sessions. When her husband was accepted at the University of North Carolina for an advanced degree, Betty got an appointment in the UNC department of psychiatry and began doing clinical work in marriage and family therapy. Within a few years, she hung out her own shingle and established a thriving private practice.

Betty's practice has changed as families have changed. She works with straight couples and gay couples, blended and step families. Modern families. She listens with intensity, and while her eyes lock, they never judge. She sees it all: anxiety, depression, problems with parents, children, addiction, and tragedies. Betty is gentle and sure. She describes her approach with her patients as precise and purposeful.

"I have a broad definition of a relationship and what constitutes family," she explains. She asks in order to learn, and to get people to talk.

Where are you hurting?
What's troubling you?
What have you tried?

Betty enjoys helping people, guiding them so they see and understand themselves more clearly. Her objective is to steer them toward "compassion and empathy for themselves," she explains. "Therein lies a lot of the healing."

Betty often begins with one of those simple open-ended questions that just invites people to talk.

What brings you here?

Then she listens. She listens for how the patient defines her problem or talks about her struggle. She "listens" with her eyes, looking for signals and signs of stress or anxiety. The color of someone's face may change. Their nose may get red. They may look like they're fighting back tears. And she might say:

What are you feeling right now?
Are you sad now?

Some will say yes. Some cry. They share a powerful, intimate moment.

"Some people will tell you the tears have been there and I haven't been able to cry them. Or I haven't been able to access this emotion. Or . . . I haven't been able to cry and I also don't sleep very well." Betty believes such an experience represents a gift for therapist and patient alike. "It's an acknowledgement the patient is feeling safe," she says, "safe enough with you to be vulnerable, to reveal themselves to you and to themselves."

Betty often follows up with one of the most effective questions you can ask, and it isn't even a question.

Tell me more.

That's what got the patient we'll call Roger to open up. Roger revealed that his marriage, which has been rocky for a few years, has gotten even worse lately. He and his wife barely talk. He had a brief affair a few months ago, but it's over now. He wasn't looking for someone to get involved with; it just happened. He knows he's at a crossroads. He is sorry about the whole situation, but he finds himself lost and confused. As for the affair, he thinks maybe it happened because his marriage left him feeling isolated and unloved. Maybe he was just vulnerable and met someone who was captivated by him when his wife was not. He doesn't know where things went wrong. He's trying to figure it out.

Now Betty can ask:

> *Did you want the marriage?*
> *Do you want to deal with it?*
> *Have you had therapy?*

She explores Roger's level of awareness, whether he is tuned in to his own feelings and to others. She wants to know how he sees this marriage and what kind of conversation he's had with himself.

> *Has your spouse been unhappy, too?*
> *What is your picture of the marriage?*
> *What's your picture of yourself as a husband?*
> *Have you said to your spouse, "I think we're in trouble. I think we need help"?*

Betty wants Roger to talk about his feelings, goals, and values.

> *How far out of integrity are you with your own vision of who you told yourself you were going to be as a husband?*
> *How does that feel?*
> *How do you talk to yourself about that?*
> *Where do you want to be with yourself now?*

Betty is following a line of inquiry she calls "accessing the internal dialogue." She wants her patients to examine and question themselves. "I might say, it sounds like you're having an internal conversation, argument, or dilemma with yourself. Who's talking and what is each part saying? Do any of those voices sound like anyone else you know?" This perspective taking looks inward. It's where her patients explore their own empathy and how they apply it to themselves and others.

Betty gets people talking—to her, to themselves, to one another. She tries to get couples face-to-face. She issues a challenge: Sit and listen for two minutes without responding or rebutting. Maintain eye contact. Try to relax. Ask questions rather than accuse. Try to understand the other person from the other person's perspective. She calls it "slow and careful and tender work."

"I often tell people you have everything you need and plenty to spare to solve this. And I say I will help you. I'm trying to empower them."

Betty asks a therapist's questions. These questions are designed to explore. They search for understanding to locate a happier, healthier person. They reflect Betty's empathy and they encourage it in her patients.

License and Limits

Empathetic questions generate some of the most personal conversations we have. They can be tricky, though, because there is no clear end point. One person's relieved revelation is another's do-not-touch secret. Knowing how and when to respect zones of guarded privacy is a tough call. It's why Betty Pristera sometimes defers to "tell me more" as she gets to know her clients. That's why Terry Gross has subjects where she follows rather than leads.

When I interview people, I feel I have license to ask just about anything. Most of the individuals I question are public figures. They expect to be asked and are skilled at telling you when you go out of bounds. Even so, there are things I won't ask about unless it is germane to their public lives or performance. I won't gratuitously ask about a person's personal life. I won't ask about pain someone has experienced just to hear them talk about it. I ask about illness or grief only if it's relevant or sheds light on a person's character.

For all these reasons, empathetic questioning requires close and constant listening for words and tone and mood. As Helen Riess and Betty Pristera noted, listening empathetically involves more than your ears because people send signals in a variety of ways about how they're feeling. They may talk freely or they may clam up, fearful of what they may discover. Reading those signals, asking openly, and listening intently is a big part of empathy itself.

CHAPTER 5

THE GENTLE INTERROGATOR
Bridging Questions

WHEN I CONDUCT AN INTERVIEW, most of the time guests show up willingly, even happily. They want to make their point, tell their story, or sell their book. They want to speak to the wider world and share their thoughts or experiences. Certainly that's true for guests who go on Terry Gross's show. She offers an audience in the millions. People make appointments to see Betty Pristera so she can question their inner selves and peel back their defenses. They want her help. But what about people who do not want to connect? How do you build bridges to people who are suspicious or distrustful, resentful or worse? What happens when someone you want to draw out doesn't want to talk? Reaching out to the suspicious or wary requires a special touch, extra patience, and bridge-building questions designed to establish a relationship and build trust with someone who may not be receptive.

You may be looking for a specific piece of information. Why is the new guy hovering in the office? You may want an explanation from a person who would rather not share it. Is your teen planning a party when you are out of town? Your approach to the "person of interest" in these conversations can become a delicate dance. But your chances of getting someone to talk will be improved if you ask the right questions in the right way—if you build bridges. You need to know:

What's going on?
What are they thinking?
Do we have a problem?

People have a lot of reasons to shut down. They may be hiding or ashamed of something. They may be suspicious of you because of your position or your history together. They may be hostile, aggrieved, or convinced that the world is against them. They may be secretive by nature. Or they may just be up to no good.

Bridging questions are intended to encourage people to talk when they don't want to. They coax information, glean detail, and assess intent and capability. They are intended for the colleague, the customer, the neighbor, the parent, the child—the suspect—who shuts down, harbors a grudge, or is thinking of doing things he or she should not do.

Bridging questions are a calculated and clever way to get people to tell you things. Sometimes I have used this approach unconsciously, when I interviewed people who were glued to their talking points, suspicious of the media, or caught up in scandal or wrongdoing. All of them were on edge, defenses raised. Few were inclined to offer information willingly. So I needed to wend my way to the relevant parts. I needed to make it easier for them to speak, holding back on the central point or toughest question until we had built a certain rapport and the moment was right. If I'd understood more about this line of inquiry—and the research that's gone into it—I might have gotten a few more scoops and stories out of those interviews.

The principles behind bridging questions support a specific and clear outcome: getting a closed person to open up. Your prospects are enhanced if you:

Know what you're after. Be clear about what you want to pursue and the nature of the problem. Have a focus and a destination in mind.

Avoid triggers. Don't start with accusations or questions that prompt defensiveness. Go instead for conversation. You want to open a channel of communication. You're in this for the long haul.

Don't accuse, ask. Start with the person's grievance and inquire about it. What's wrong? What's unfair? Then ask about rationale and motivations.

Affirm and validate. Walking someone across a bridge takes them farther than pushing them off a cliff. You want answers, background, and insight, so you want to encourage discussion. Guide and affirm. Offer rewards. Look for small ways to move across the bridge. The main thing is to get your subject talking. Be patient. This may take a while.

Get Them Talking

In this chapter, I introduce you to someone whose experience, insight, and work offer a travel guide to the toughest and most reluctant human terrain. He teaches how to question the most vexing characters. Though the examples he offers are extreme, the tactics are not. If you've ever tried to get answers from someone who won't open up or who you think is harboring secrets or sitting on some bad stuff, you know how important these questions can be.

> *What motivates you?*
> *What are you thinking?*
> *Are you dangerous?*

Barry Spodak is an expert in threat assessment. He has studied people who keep the darkest, most dangerous secrets. He knows how to talk to them and he has developed protocols for questioning them and building bridges so they will open up, even a little. He wants to get them to reveal their thoughts and intentions so he can determine whether they are on "a path to violence." But what Barry has learned on the fringes can be applied to the mainstream. His tools can be put to work in everyday places.

Barry and I have known one another for years. His gentle demeanor belies his work on the dark side of humanity. Barry trains FBI and Secret Service agents and U.S. Marshals in questioning potential serial killers, terrorists, or would-be presidential assassins *before* they act. Sometimes he dresses up—beard, tattoos, earrings—to give his agent-students a living, breathing suspect so they can role-play the conversation. Barry can be a white supremacist, a Middle Eastern arms merchant, or a Christian or Muslim extremist. His disguises would make his favorite Hollywood makeup artist proud.

To Barry, everyone is a puzzle. Some people are just more complex, more mysterious, and more urgent to put together than others. He's been drawn to them all his life, dramatically discovering this line of work when he was a young graduate student in Washington, D.C., in the late 1970s. His focus was on violent criminals who had been declared not guilty by reason of insanity. His studies involved fieldwork at St. Elizabeth's Hospital—in its day, one of the premier psychiatric facilities in the country. To get locked up in a psych ward, someone had to be judged a danger to themselves or others. The challenge was how to determine if someone actually posed a threat. There was little research at the time, so psychologists and law enforcement alike struggled for a consistent approach to threat assessment.

Barry's responsibilities at St Elizabeth's included leading group therapy sessions. One day, a newcomer joined the group. He sat off to the side, watching, listening, but seldom participating. He seemed subdued, quiet, and innocuous enough. He had no previous history of mental illness. There was no outward indication that he posed a threat to anyone. Yet everyone knew the stark reality: He had tried to kill the president of the United States.

John Hinckley Jr. had pulled the trigger six times on his .22 caliber revolver outside the Washington Hilton Hotel on March 30, 1981, as President Ronald Reagan exited the building and made his way to the motorcade. The first bullet went into the head of White House Press

Secretary James Brady. The second struck police officer Thomas Delahanty in the back of the neck. The third hit the window of a building across the street. Special Agent in Charge Jerry Parr pushed Reagan into the limousine as a fourth bullet hit Secret Service Agent Timothy McCarthy in the abdomen as he spread his body over Reagan. The fifth hit the side of the limousine. The sixth bullet ricocheted off the limousine and hit the president under his left arm and entered his body, lodging in his lung, one inch from his heart. The president nearly died as a result of a staph infection that followed.

Hinckley had been obsessed with the actress Jodie Foster. He had stalked her when she was at Yale. He thought killing the president would get her attention and impress her. A jury found Hinckley not guilty by reason of insanity. He was twenty-six years old when he joined Barry's group therapy session for the first time.

In therapy, Hinckley said little. On occasion he would mention something about life inside the institution or about other patients or the staff. Barry recalled that Hinckley seemed scared of the other patients; he didn't talk much to anyone in the early days. Barry tried to draw him out.

What was he thinking?
Could he be reached?

Off to the side, in one-on-one conversations, Hinckley offered a few words and opened up just a little. "He would talk to me after group therapy," Barry recalled. "Hinckley thought we were about the same age so he didn't feel threatened by me." It's not hard to see why. Barry is soft spoken, his voice gentle and mellifluous. He listens with his eyes. He used those attributes to slowly develop some rapport with the young man who nearly killed a president.

"I was able to sit with him outside the building and I got a little of his history and was able to better elicit his story of how he came to do what he did." Barry won't provide details out of respect for Hinckley's privacy, but he learned that a deliberate, respectful process of asking and providing a sympathetic ear could prompt a would-be assassin to talk.

Solving Puzzles

Over the years, Barry built on his fascination with human puzzles. He developed protocols and practices for how to talk to and question potential assassins, terrorists, school shooters, and disgruntled employees. He became an expert in threat assessment. His approach is proactive and his purpose is clear: Talk to people before they act and elicit information to determine whether they are on a path to violence. He teaches what to ask, when to respond, and how to listen.

It's worth pointing out that Barry's methods do not involve the good-cop, bad-cop approach you see in the movies, where one interrogator intimidates and threatens while the other offers the sympathetic ear. He does not teach in-your-face screaming, where a questioner tries to frighten or intimidate someone into opening up. And he has nothing to do with "enhanced interrogation" of the sort Americans used in Afghanistan and Iraq, intended to crush the spirit and force the subject to talk.

Barry teaches "rights respecting" questioning, which most experts say is the most effective way to get a hostile person to open up. His objective is to lower a person's defenses and move his or her brain out of red alert territory. His questions are framed to generate conversation, however halting, as a means of establishing trust and building a dynamic that will coax information from the most reticent personalities.

Strip away the prime-time drama from Barry's characters and you have a screenplay that might feature your family, your friends, or your workplace. Someone is keeping a secret. Someone is plotting. Someone isn't telling you what you need to know. If you can use bridging questions in the right way, you can get people to talk, draw them out, and get a picture of the path they are traveling. Step one is to ratchet down the tension.

Barry adheres to a psychological theory, developed by Nobel Prize–winning psychologist Daniel Kahneman, that posits two "systems" in which the human brain operates. *System One* is a sort of low gear; it goes anywhere and allows us to make decisions easily and come up with ready answers. Consider it your brain's autopilot. It goes on when your surroundings and reference points are familiar. If someone asks you what's two plus two, you answer "four" automatically, without effort. It takes no effort to come up with the answer. In System One, which Kahneman calls "cognitive ease," we feel relaxed, comfortable, and in control. A questioner might put someone in System One by asking about the weather or an article of clothing, or even by offering a cup of coffee. A warm and familiar gesture, the coffee becomes a reassuring prop.

System Two triggers the brain's overdrive, making it spin faster, work harder, and use more oxygen. System Two is a response to the unfamiliar, the complex, the difficult or frightening. A tough math problem or contentious situation can put us in this state. You stop, react, scramble for a response.

A brain in System Two is on alert, with its guard up. Unfamiliar or unfriendly surroundings can shift the mind into this gear. We begin watching every word we say. What's four hundred thirty-five divided by nine? Did you take my bottle of gin?

System Two is likely the state your teen is in if he thinks you are accusing or judging him. It's the state you are in if your boss gives you a harsh performance review. It's how just about every suspect is reacting during questioning.

Barry teaches agents how to put their subjects' brains in System One, into low gear, as much as possible. He tells his students to start with questions the interviewee is comfortable addressing, even if the questions are not relevant to the issue at hand. Ask about a common experience or a part of the interviewee's life that is known and not controversial.

Suppose an agent is paying a visit to Joseph, whose name surfaced in an investigation. For now, Joseph is being treated as a source, not a suspect. Walking into the living room, the agent notices a piece of art on the wall.

Nice painting, who did that?

Assuming the agent is not there to talk about art theft, the question may serve as an icebreaker—an acknowledgment, even a compliment. The focus on the art lets Joseph speak about something familiar, on his own turf. The agent should listen closely, Barry counsels, and if she hears Joseph open up, she should ask some more about the painting to generate a few minutes of easy conversation, to move Joseph's brain back to cognitive ease.

Those of us who aren't federal agents use this method in conversation, consciously or not. We use icebreakers to introduce ourselves, to establish a rapport, to launch conversation with interesting small talk.

Imagine that you're a manager in an insurance firm. Anna, one of your employees, comes to your office for her annual review. A couple of coworkers have complained about disparaging remarks she has made behind people's backs. You want her to stop, but you need to know what she's got on her mind in case it points to a deeper problem. She's on guard. You recall seeing a new computer on her desk. You ask:

How's the new computer working out?

"It's really fast," she says. "This one doesn't crash. And it's about time. That upgrade was long overdue."

It's not much, but you've got Anna talking.

"That's great," you say. "Don't you love that touch screen?" You can see Anna's shoulders release from their defensive shrug. She's not exactly happy to be with you, but at least you've established that she likes her new computer.

You're busy, and you need to move Anna toward the issue that has come to your attention. But take your time, Barry advises. Don't kick her into System Two with direct questions just yet. Stay with the computer angle for a minute.

How did you decide on that computer?

This question is intended to evoke a different kind of answer. "How" questions ask for explanation and background. They encourage stories.

Barry tells his FBI and Secret Service students to understand that the human brain is wired for stories. It's how we learn and how we remember. It's how we engage and pass along our experience and our history. Cave paintings were stories. The Bible and the Quran and the Torah tell stories. We put our kids to bed telling stories. Alibis and confessions are stories.

If Barry were Anna's boss, he would play off her comments and ask:

Do most people choose that computer? Is it a popular choice?

He is listening hard for "entry points" to turn the conversation with Anna to the story he wants to hear.

Yes, she might say, most people select that model. She read extensively about her computer before choosing it. That's how she does all her work, thoroughly and diligently. Here's where her story offers an entry point.

"I use my computer differently," she says. "That's what makes me more effective in my work. More than Al up in accounts payable who has the other model."

Anna is now "differentiating" herself, Barry explains. By comparing herself to Al in accounts payable, Anna is offering a clue that an astute questioner can pick up on. Something sets her apart. This provides an entry point. Barry would ask about that.

Really? What's going on with Al?

Anna might start to describe how her coworker handled a situation recently and how other people weighed in and what happened. As she tells the story, she provides more entry points, more opportunities to ask.

Catching the entry points requires focused listening to form follow-up questions that move the story along and elicit details. You can recognize an entry point by actively listening for an observation or a complaint that resonates with the story you're after. A flash of anger or an expression of regret can be an entry point. Use it to your advantage. In essence, you are conducting a sort of interrogational game of chess, hearing answers, forming questions, but thinking several moves ahead. So you ask strategically. You know where you want the conversation to go, but you need your opponent to make the moves that get there. Your questions are only as good as the answers they provoke.

Affirm and Acknowledge

To keep his subjects talking, on track, and in System One, Barry uses periodic "micro-affirmations." When he hears something relevant or that he wants to learn more about, he signals his interest in almost imperceptible movements, gestures, or sounds. He might lean forward and offer a slight nod or a barely audible "uh-huh." These micro-affirmations reinforce without interrupting or distracting. They signal that Barry is engaged and sympathetic. "One of the things we keep in mind," Barry says, "is that people who are angry rarely find others who listen." A questioner who listens provides a welcome refuge.

As the conversation unwinds, Barry also offers "rewards" or a brief acknowledgement. "That's really interesting," he will say. "I hadn't thought about it that way," or "That's a good point." Citing neuroscience research and his own experience, Barry told me that when you give people something, they are inclined to give something back. "I try to give them words back that make them feel that I am really appreciative of their intellect or their insight or whatever they need to hear. That will be the reward."

Questions Without Question Marks

This book is all about asking. But as we've seen, some questions work best when they don't end in a question mark.

Tell me more.
Explain that to me.

These command-questions serve as open-ended invitations for a subject to pause, reflect, and provide more detail. I think of them as questions without question marks. They ask without asking. They convey interest and, when stated in the right tone, accompanied by open body language, they offer affirmation and validation, which Barry says is so important to reduce barriers and generate cognitive ease. Questions without question marks can feel less threatening, less like an interrogation.

In my interviewing, I have found that this technique provides breathing space for the other person, a break from the usual Q&A pattern. I put my pen down, lean forward, and knit my brow in what I intend to be a visibly curious expression. It's my way of saying I'm hooked, fascinated by what I'm hearing. I want my companion to know that I am not just a good audience, but a rapt listener. I might say:

Go on.
That's remarkable.
Fascinating.

Barry counsels his agents to turn questions into statements whenever they can. The technique encourages conversation, especially if someone is trying to conceal something. He offers a real-world scenario: The feds have intercepted a long, rambling email from a man who calls himself Lucas. The email vents at the government, rails at Washington, and then, in thinly disguised language, threatens the president. Agents track Lucas down and bring him in for questioning. He is angry, curt, and agitated. Though he has no criminal record, his comments on his social media accounts suggest a disgruntled, antigovernment loner.

Barry would *not* start by asking, "Why have you been sending threatening emails?" Nor would he ask, "Do you intend to kill the president?" These questions would only shut Lucas down. Instead, Barry asks one of his questions without a question mark. He says:

It sounds like some of the things the president has done have really
*   gotten you annoyed.*

Lucas sits up. "Annoyed? Are you kidding? Of course. I'm annoyed . . . I'm more than annoyed."

Barry listens intently. He wants Lucas to feel he's being heard. Like a hostage negotiator, he wants to keep the conversation going, thinking ahead, moving in on the issues. He zeros in on what's bothering Lucas and poses another question without a question mark:

A lot of people agree with you. (Pause.) *Tell me about that.*

"Well, of course people agree with me. They're angry! The guy is ruining the country. And I'll tell you how he's doing it . . ." Now Lucas is on a roll. He's telling a story.

Angry, alienated people may believe they see and understand things that others do not. By saying, "A lot of people agree with you," Barry offers Lucas a measure of validation. Not an endorsement of his point of view, but the recognition that Lucas has company. Barry avoids showing disapproval or disagreement. He "normalizes" the conversation, creating the appearance that he understands, along with the hint that he may even be an ally.

I hope you don't encounter Lucas. But you can use these "questions without question marks" in almost any conversation with someone who is reluctant to speak or hesitant to provide more than a cursory response. These questions offer affirmation. They suggest the questioner is a receptive audience. They serve to promote dialogue that will lead to more entry points to explore.

Echo Questions

I use another kind of affirmation that fully embraces its question mark. I call them "echo questions." I ask them in almost every type of interview because they are so clear and effective. They almost always prompt the interviewee to talk more and go deeper. These, too, are effective bridge-building questions. Echo questions enable me to use the other person's own words for emphasis and as a follow-up question. I add inflection to suit the mood—sympathy, surprise, and humor.

Henry says, "The way they treated me just made me want to scream."
You ask your echo question. "Scream?"

Rita says, "I don't know why I even try anymore. They are so incompetent."
You say, "Incompetent?"

In most cases, those one-word echo questions will lead to more detail and explanation.

Your six-year-old comes home from school with a note from the teacher saying your child swiped a banana from a classmate at lunch. You ask what happened.

"The lunch room was really noisy and Katie was being mean. So I took her banana."

Echo question: "You *took* it?"

"Yes, I took it. But I didn't steal it, I just took it. She was saying bad things about me and I didn't like it."

Life is simple at six. Now you have a teachable moment. You can explain that we don't "take" things from other people's lunch trays, even if we're annoyed at them.

Barry teaches this technique as part of what he calls "reflective listening." He tells his agent-students they must be fully present if they are going to catch these comments on the fly. And in threat assessment, the stakes are huge.

Back to "Lucas" and his threatening emails. He wrote, "The president is ruining the country." Lucas says it again in his interview. Upon hearing the words, an astute agent echoes them back.

Ruining the country?

"Yes! Ruining the country. He's letting in the wrong kind of people; they're stealing our money and taking away our freedoms. Something's got to be done!"

The next question acknowledges the burden of Lucas's insight. It affirms and then echoes his last point.

This must be tough for you to live with.
Do you have ideas about what should be done?

Because the questioner is trying to determine whether Lucas is on a path to violence, this exchange could be a critical turning point in the conversation. Lucas might reveal what he thinks should be done, whether he knows other people who feel the same way, maybe even whether he's prepared to take action himself.

Echo questions and reflective listening leverage the words you hear to extract more of the thinking behind them. They serve as punctuation points in questioning to seize a moment or a thought, highlight it, and invite additional detail and discussion.

Build the Bridge

Bridge-building questions work best when people are at cognitive ease and feel they have a receptive audience. You can achieve this effect with questions (with or without question marks) by making use of words or expressions you have just heard, by listening for entry points, and by careful affirmation of difficult or irrational thoughts. You build the bridge, one piece, one question at a time. You plot a deliberate, careful course, knowing that this bridge will take time to construct and that there will likely be setbacks along the way.

CHAPTER 6

FOR THE RECORD
Confrontational Questions

SOMETIMES YOU CAN'T BUILD BRIDGES. You're not looking for empathy and you're not looking for trust. You just need an answer. You have to hold someone's feet to the fire, stare straight into their eyes, and ask what they knew, when they knew it, or what they *did*, *said*, or *intended*. You want a clear answer to a straight-up question. You need to pin down someone's role or responsibility, complicity or culpability. You want accountability.

There are plenty of times when people need to be confronted and held to account. We do it with our children in order to teach them responsibility, set boundaries, and demonstrate the consequences of their actions. We want our politicians to be accountable because they hold a public trust. We think corporations should be accountable because they should do more than just make money. We hold one another to account if we think there has been wrongdoing, bad behavior, hypocrisy, or incompetence: Perhaps you suspect a colleague has been cheating on her expense accounts, the police chief may be turning a blind eye to corrupt cops, a relative is siphoning money from Aunt Sophie's retirement account, or a partner is acting suspiciously.

Is this your handwriting?
Were you aware that this was happening?

Confrontation and accountability questions put issues on the table and demand answers for the record. They air a grievance, level an accusation, and reinforce the rules of acceptable behavior. Accountability questions are asked in public or in private, in the glare of the lights or in the shadows of the most intimate relationships. They are necessary, but they can be risky business. The principles of confrontational questioning reflect the realities of this high-voltage exchange. They are best approached when you:

Know your goal. Set it and stick with it. Do you want an acknowledgment, an admission, an expression of regret or remorse, or a confession? Plot your question trajectory with your objective in mind. Anticipate what it will take to get there.

Know your facts. Be sure they are complete and accurate. You need a solid foundation of information if you are going to accuse or confront. This is key to asking the right questions, anticipating the answers, and avoiding embarrassing mistakes.

Frame your questions surgically. Precise answers are elicited with precise questions. Use direct questions. Frame them to support your case. Listen closely and ask again if you don't get a direct answer.

Care about the question. If you're going into battle, you should be more than a mercenary. Your passion and your commitment will elevate the intensity and poignancy of the questions you ask. Craft your questions to project moral authority. Take the high road.

Expect a defensive, evasive, or confrontational response. People don't like to be called on the carpet and may ignore the question, duck the answer, or attack the messenger rather than acknowledge their fault or flaw. Be ready to rumble. Be prepared with a follow-up if this happens.

Succeeding in the high stakes world of confrontational questioning requires engaging all of these principles so that you can be a worthy adversary. You will be tested on several levels.

Care to Listen

Caring about your cause brings commitment. Being knowledgeable conveys authority. Listening closely provides opportunity. If you're going to stand up to the mayor or to the neighborhood bully, you need the courage of your convictions and the muscle of facts. And you want to use the clock to your advantage.

CNN's Anderson Cooper is adept at using all of these skills. He is approachable, but he is tough and unflinching when he leans on someone for what they've done or said. We met at his home, a renovated old firehouse in lower Manhattan, to talk about these types of questions. Decorated with antiques, collector's items from his famous Vanderbilt ancestors, and other gems—I especially liked the eight-foot black bear looming over the living room—the house is a mix of old-world royalty and hipster urban retreat. Not far from the commanding portrait of Cooper's great grandfather, railroad and shipping magnate Commodore Vanderbilt, we settled in for a conversation about how questions, listening, and confrontation connect.

Cooper and I overlapped a bit at CNN. He always impressed me with his intelligence, range and sincerity. His work has taken him from epic disasters around the world and mud hut sanctuaries in Africa's embattled hellholes to stage-managed presidential debates in America's heartland and the most glamorous places on the planet. He is empathetic by nature. He told me that he tries to be a "capable recipient" of everything he hears. Respecting silence matters to him. He got involved in mindfulness meditation to become more "present."

His interest in holding people to account is an acquired skill. "Confrontation doesn't come naturally," he acknowledged. But he believes that public officials are seldom held to account in a thoughtful and thorough manner. When he's got facts that stand in stark contrast to the reality of a situation or what a person has said or done, he feels compelled to challenge openly.

He doesn't like confrontational interviews driven by opinion or attitude. "I find them circular and ultimately unsatisfying. But an interview where you have facts that oppose and contradict what a person has said, and you are presenting those facts to them, you're challenging them basically on something they said—those are the interviews I now enjoy and are important," he told me. "These are the hardest interviews" because they require so much preparation and "you have to be armed with what is true." Cooper has refined his approach.

"I used to make the mistake of thinking I had to cover everything. I now realize in those interviews, those confrontational interviews, that you focus on one or two points." He knows the clock is ticking and his adversary is calculating. "The other person often relies on the time constraints and on you ultimately just backing off and moving on. But if you just refuse to move on and are willing to ask the same question over and over again, when they're not answering, it reveals something else about them."

Confrontational questioning often requires assertive interruption or repetition in order to make it as difficult as possible for your adversary to change the subject, dodge the question or run out the clock.

Cooper's defining interview in this respect took place in the midst of disaster after Hurricane Katrina in 2005. He had been on-site for a few days, had seen the flooding, and talked to everyone from citizens to first responders and elected officials. On this day, he'd been out with a recovery team from the Federal Emergency Management Agency (FEMA). They had gone to a flooded home where the dead were still lying in their living room. The stench, the images, the loss were all fresh in his mind. They collided with images from other places where he'd seen bodies left to rot—Somalia, Rwanda, Sarajevo. But this was America. This was home.

How was this happening?
Who was responsible?

As he went on the air for an interview with Louisiana senator Mary Landrieu, Cooper had a hyperaware sense of the sounds around him— flies buzzing and plastic sheets whipping in the wind—the sounds of neglect, incompetence, and prolonged suffering. He got right to it, asking Landrieu:

*Does the federal government bear responsibility for what is
   happening now?*
Should they apologize for what is happening now?

Landrieu dodged.

There would be "plenty of time" to discuss the issues of "when and
how and what and if . . . ," she said. Everyone understood the situation
was serious. She wanted to thank people—the president, the military,
the first responders, leaders who had visited, fellow senators. Maybe
Anderson hadn't heard the news yet, she droned on, but the Senate had
passed a supplemental $10 billion emergency relief bill.

After nearly a full minute of this, Cooper jumped in.

"Senator, excuse me for interrupting. For the last four days I've been
seeing dead bodies in the street. And to listen to politicians thanking
each other and complimenting each other, you know I've got to tell you,
there are a lot of people here who are very upset and very angry and very
frustrated. And when they hear politicians thanking one another, it kind
of cuts them the wrong way right now because literally—there was a
body on the streets of this town yesterday being eaten by rats because
this woman had been lying in the streets for forty-eight hours and there
are not enough facilities to take her up." Then he asked:

Do you get the anger that is out here?

Landrieu, stilted and robotic, sounded like she was reading from a
script. "Anderson, I have the anger inside of me . . ."

Who are you angry at?

"I'm not angry at anyone . . ."

She never directly addressed the question of who was responsible for
the failure in New Orleans.

"Being in a place like that, all the bullshit is stripped away," Cooper
told me. "It's like the flesh is ripped off and everything is raw and
exposed. I just got angry . . . it just seemed wrong. It just seemed

inappropriate." He had been listening for an answer and instead got evasion and excuses.

Cooper brought together firsthand knowledge of the story with a sense of moral outrage. His questions demanded accountability. Landrieu's answers, which were shockingly unresponsive, only accentuated the ineptitude of government at a moment of crisis. Landrieu's performance tarnished her reputation; Cooper's performance elevated his. But Cooper's approach highlighted a pillar of confrontational questioning: persistence. He interrupted when Landrieu tried to make an irrelevant speech instead of offering a direct response. He returned to his question and asked again. He applied righteous indignation to emphasize the moral certitude that motivated his questioning. In the end, Landrieu acknowledged nothing, but the record was clear.

Unintended Consequences

Even with extensive knowledge, preparation, and skin in the game, confrontational questioning can go off the rails. I learned this the hard way, in a very public setting, when I interviewed one of the world's most controversial and charismatic figures.

It was one of the strangest interviews I've done. I "presided" at the prestigious Council on Foreign Relations in Washington, D.C., in front of a live audience and a cluster of cameras from around the world. My task was to ask Yasser Arafat, leader of the Palestinian Liberation Organization, a few questions and then open the discussion to audience Q&A. Some people still considered him a terrorist. Others viewed him as a freedom fighter. It was a challenging assignment.

As we gathered, the Mideast was again in turmoil. Another Palestinian uprising, an intifada, had ignited the territories. The world bore witness to the sad story of the region's endless conflict and suffering— this time, through pictures of young protesters, children in many cases, throwing rocks and using slingshots against well-armed Israeli troops. In the most searing image, cameras captured the fatal shooting of a twelve-year-old boy, Muhammad al-Durrah, as his father tried to protect him with his bare hands while they huddled behind a metal barrel.

Mixed with the outrage directed at both sides were calls for Arafat to encourage Palestinian children to stay off the streets and away from the hostilities. But Arafat was silent. Israeli leaders and others accused him of actually wanting more victims, more incendiary images to wave around in an effort to pressure Israel and rally global opinion.

I wanted to ask Arafat about those children. They were too young to be dying in his streets, too young to be traded for propaganda points. I felt he needed to answer his critics.

Why had he been silent?
Why didn't he protect his children?
How did he respond to criticism from around the world?

I knew he would bristle at the accusation. I had worked the phones, talking to people who knew Arafat and the Middle East to figure out the best way to frame the questions so he'd actually answer. Acknowledge his stature, the experts told me. Play to his influence and his ego. Invoke the protective instinct a father feels when his child is in danger. In a region so poisoned by history, frame the question to look forward, not back. Appeal to his sense of destiny. All of it was sound advice. None of it worked.

We were seated at the front of a room on a small platform that was just big enough for our two green-upholstered armchairs and a coffee table with two glasses and a pitcher of water. Arafat wore his trademark kaffiyeh, a checkered head wrap that draped nearly to his waist. The room was packed. *USA Today* described the crowd as the "crème de la crème of the U.S. foreign policy establishment."

I began with some innocuous questions about Arafat's meeting that day with President Clinton, the situation on the ground, and prospects for resuming negotiations with the Israelis. Just before I went to audience questions, I turned to the issue of the children. Reflecting the advice I'd been given, I credited Arafat with being the "longtime leader" of the Palestinian people. I sought to acknowledge his influence by invoking "many" in America and the Middle East who said he had an "opportunity" to act. I made reference to his authority and tried to connect it to the future and the children by saying he could call on people "to stand down . . ." I hadn't gotten the full question out of my mouth when he erupted.

"We are animals?" he shouted at me. I continued, intent on getting a response to the question I'd asked.

"Specifically, the children . . ."

He leaped out of his chair, shaking his finger. "You want me to treat our people as animals?" He appeared to be on the verge of storming out of the room.

"Sir," I asserted, "I merely asked a question . . ."

I crossed my legs and extended them to fill the space between that coffee table and us, blocking his most obvious escape route. After a few seconds that felt like forever, he sat down, glowering. We continued.

It was an especially awkward moment because I was meant to be both questioner and gracious host. Arafat was a "guest" of the Council, whose events were supposed to be thoughtful and dignified. But this question about the children had to be asked, and asked unapologetically. I should have pushed harder and worried less about civility and propriety. I didn't want to lose him, though. By now, it was time for questions from the audience.

One person took up where I left off. He came from AIPAC of all places, the American-Israeli lobby. He asked my question again, this time employing a highly effective technique in confrontational questioning: He invoked an impeccable third party. This tactic shifts the burden of assertion from the questioner to someone with expertise, stature, or moral authority. In this case, the impeccable third party was the Queen of Sweden, who had very publicly commented on the use of Palestinian children in the uprising.

"As a mother, I'm very worried about this . . . the children should not take part," she had said.

Q FROM AUDIENCE: *Mr. Chairman, could you comment on the Queen of Sweden's public condemnation of the use of children by the Palestinian leadership in fighting against Israel?*

ARAFAT: *Use of children?*

Q: *I said the Queen of Sweden's public condemnation of the use by the Palestinian leadership of children in the fight against Israel.*

ARAFAT: *Use of the children? I cannot accept this statement. I'm not using our children. We are working very hard for the future . . . Are you against this?* (Pauses for a moment.) *You know, someone from AIPAC should have apologized for killing all the Palestinian children. This would have been the high road.*

Arafat had no intention of addressing the question directly, whether it came from me or anybody else. But the encounter served an important purpose: it put him on the spot—and on the record—for the entire world to see. His supporters would see his anger as defiance; his antagonists would see petulance. I still believe it was an important exchange. It illustrated that confrontational questions set an agenda and create a historical record.

The exchange also showed that no matter how much you plan or how compelling the "impeccable third party" may be, you can run into a defensive and angry buzz-saw response when you accuse or confront. People will bluster, bloviate, or evade. You need a strategy to assert control that goes beyond crossing your legs and hoping the person doesn't storm out of the room. Sometimes you can't worry about being polite.

Demanding Answers

When you adopt a true adversarial approach, you raise the stakes. Asking with righteous indignation can quickly create enemies. Jorge Ramos has no problem with that. He's not trying to make friends.

One of the most famous Latinos in the United States, Ramos is a powerful and principled anchorman for the Spanish-language network Univision. He has been called the Hispanic Walter Cronkite—except Ramos has more than a million Twitter followers and goes toe to toe with world leaders in ways Cronkite would have found unthinkable. Ramos has gotten roughed up, shut down, and thrown out because he relishes confrontation in the service of accountability. He sees it as the foundation of democracy, transparency, and legitimacy.

"I feel a mission," he told me. "The most social responsibility we have is to confront those who are in power. That creates a balance of power in our country and our world."

Ramos is well aware that his confrontational style may infuriate and alienate the person he's interviewing, especially if it's someone in power. "I always assume I will never talk to that person again," Ramos says.

But even Ramos was surprised when he got thrown out of a roomful of reporters as he tried to question the most unlikely of presidential candidates, billionaire businessman Donald Trump. Having concluded that Trump's position on immigration was bigoted, ill-informed, and indefensible, Ramos showed up ready to hurl barbed questions and take on the man who was leading in the polls and would become the Republican nominee.

Trump made headlines when he declared that Mexicans were "bringing drugs. They're bringing crime. They're rapists. And some, I assume, are good people." He called for a wall along the Mexican border. He promised that if elected, he'd deport 11 million undocumented immigrants. He said children born in the United States to undocumented immigrants shouldn't be U.S. citizens, though the Constitution grants anyone born in the United States full and instant citizenship. For Jorge Ramos, a Mexican American who immigrated to the United States as a young man, these were insulting positions he wanted to challenge directly.

At a crowded news conference in Dubuque, Iowa, Ramos stood.

"I have a question about immigration . . ." That was about all he got a chance to say.

"You weren't called. Sit down," Trump barked.

Ramos wouldn't budge.

Trump turned to call on someone else, but Ramos persisted.

"I'm a reporter, an immigrant, and a citizen," Ramos said, "I have the right to ask a question."

Trump signaled a burly security guard to usher Ramos out of the room.

Ramos protested loudly. "Don't touch me, sir. You cannot touch me. I have the right to ask a question."

In all his years confronting Latin American dictators and strongmen, he had never been ejected from a news conference.

After several minutes and some prodding from other reporters, Trump changed his mind and allowed Ramos back in.

"Good to have you back," Trump said with a straight face.

"Here's the problem with your immigration plan," Ramos stated. "It's full of empty promises. You cannot deport 11 million undocumented immigrants. You cannot deny citizenship to the children of these immigrants . . ."

Trump jumped in.

"That's not right," he asserted, saying that an "act of Congress" could change the status of the "anchor babies" born in the United States to undocumented migrant parents.

Ramos tried another tactic, asking, "How are you going to build a 1,900-mile wall?"

"Very easy. I'm a builder," Trump said dismissively.

And on it went for nearly five minutes. Ramos asserting, arguing, asking, Trump dodging.

Looking back on it, Ramos said he probably got thrown out because Trump was unnerved by the basic premise of his question—that Trump's policy was built on "empty promises"—and aggravated by Ramos's decision to stand. But theatrics are often part of confrontation.

"We knew we had to do two things as journalists," Ramos explained to me. "First, to stand up. If you ask a question sitting down, it would be a completely different balance of power. And second, we knew that I was only going to have a few seconds to ask the question. I purposely made the decision that I was going to continue asking the question regardless of what he was going to be doing."

Ramos concluded that the spectacle was worth it. He made his point and put the issues on the record for all to see.

"I did my job as a journalist and the audience—especially Latinos—know exactly what kind of candidate Trump is. The big lesson is, never stop asking questions. I would have failed if I had sat down at that press conference in Dubuque, Iowa," he said. "I did not sit down. I didn't go. I did not shut up."

Confronting Power

Ramos's confrontational style is deeply rooted in his experience and youth. His autocratic father left little room for discussion or dissent and had rigid ideas about what his boy would become—an engineer, an architect, a doctor, or a lawyer. But young Jorge had no interest in those fields. Making matters worse, he regarded his Catholic school as a straitjacket. Home was often a battlefield.

"Growing up, I learned to confront the most powerful man in my world, my father," he said.

At school, he challenged another father, the priest to whom the students had to confess their sins. This priest was also in charge of discipline—often harsh, physical discipline. Ramos saw this as an incredible abuse of power.

Why do you do this?
How is this moral?

He challenged the priest directly, telling him "It wasn't right for an old man to hit a small child."

As Ramos grew older, he became acutely aware of another abuse of power: his country's corrupt politics. Again, he felt a duty to question it and expose those responsible. But, again, he collided with a culture that considered itself above challenge and certainly not accountable to a young reporter. In his first job in Mexican television, Ramos clashed with his bosses and with the censors who wanted the stories told their way. At age 24, Ramos moved to Los Angeles to study journalism at UCLA and pursue a career in the United States. He has been asking his questions ever since. He asked Fidel Castro why there was no democracy in Cuba. He asked Venezuelan strongman Hugo Chavez about his abuses of power and broken promises. He grilled former Mexican president Carlos Salinas about his role in the assassination of a political rival. He asked Colombian president Ernesto Samper about allegations that he was on the take from Colombian drug lords.

He did not make many friends. After one assignment, Ramos returned to the office to find a chilling gift—a funeral spray of flowers. They had been delivered anonymously shortly after he received a death threat. But Ramos wants to make people in power feel the heat, to challenge them directly on their broken promises, flagrant contradictions, and outright lies.

Ramos counsels that confrontational questioning must be approached from a position of strength. "Questions can be used as weapons. If you're going to confront someone in power, there has to be an element of aggressiveness." You must have the courage of your convictions and realize this isn't a popularity contest. "Whenever I go into an interview I assume two things: If I don't ask the question no one else will, and I'm always assuming this may be my last exchange."

Ramos believes we should be asking for much more accountability. We should demand it at every level of our lives. "We all have the right—the responsibility—to challenge and question powerful people."

An Audience Helps

You don't need a television show to be effective when asking for accountability. If you have the basics—solid information, a clear objective to your questioning, and enough spine and moral indignation to stand up to authority—you can have impact, especially if you understand your platform and know your audience. Invoking community is one of the surest ways to give more heft to your case and more edge to your questions.

Thomas Wilson's questions were powerful. But it was the audience around him that made his appeal impossible to ignore. Wilson was a specialist with the Tennessee National Guard. He was serving in Iraq at a time when large numbers of U.S. service members were dying as a result of improvised explosive devices—IEDs—that regularly ripped through poorly protected Humvees and other vehicles. At a gathering that was supposed to be a pep rally—the *New York Times* described it as a "morale-lifting town hall discussion with Iraq-bound troops"—Wilson raised his hand and asked the visiting secretary of defense, Donald Rumsfeld, a pair of right-between-the-eyes questions.

> *Why do we soldiers have to dig through local landfills for pieces*
> *of scrap metal and compromised ballistic glass to up-armor our*
> *vehicles?*
> *Why don't we have those resources readily available to us?*

The place burst into applause. Wilson was asking what everyone in the room was thinking. Rumsfeld was caught off guard and, uncharacteristically, at a loss for words.

"Now, settle down, settle down," he told the crowd. "Hell, I'm an old man, it's early in the morning, and I'm gathering my thoughts here."

"It was highly unusual for soldiers to dare to confront Mr. Rumsfeld directly," the *Times* pointed out. But Wilson's questions were poignant and accurate and brilliantly framed. They drew attention to the problem of under-armored vehicles and increased the pressure to fix the problem. Wilson's platform—a troop town hall in Kuwait—was compelling. His community was reinforcing. He invoked the crowd and painted a vivid word picture of the problem. He gave it a moral undertone and framed it as a shameful betrayal of those who were doing the fighting and dying. And it wasn't a speech; it was a question.

The Pentagon felt the heat and amped up efforts to provide the armor the vehicles needed.

Whether at a town hall or a staff meeting, confronting a powerful person is not easy. But having a community on your side creates an alliance. Your questions become the group's questions, harder to dismiss as the ranting of a malcontent and easier to amplify because of the implied voices ready to join you. If you've done your homework, are prepared to stand up to the pressure of the encounter, and have crafted your questions so that you succinctly express the problem and the challenge, you can take the high ground and demand answers.

No Way Out

The situations, personalities, and dynamics of this line of inquiry vary widely. But whether you are confronting a politician who has broken a promise or a salesman who has ripped you off, a student who has cheated on an exam or an employee who has padded an expense report, you should prepare for an evasive or confrontational response.

Effective confrontational questioners have to be fast and uncompromising listeners. It's what good lawyers do in a courtroom and what good interviewers do in front of a camera. They pick up on voice tone and swoop in on hesitation. They shut down attempts to filibuster or self-aggrandize. They keep the laser aimed at the core issue they're after.

I've talked a lot about open-ended questions, those broad, nonthreatening inquiries that invite people to answer as they wish and go where they want. Accountability questioning is different. You want precision. You want to pin someone down. You don't want to ask a question that lets someone off the hook or invites a speech she can use to obscure the argument or change the subject. Often, questions that elicit one-word answers can be the most effective crowbars to the truth. Yes-no questions.

You were late yesterday. Is that correct?
Did you call when you knew you were going to be late?
Did you think about the consequences of being late?

I wanted to explore how lawyers apply this yes-no strategy, so I called on Ted Olson, the great conservative attorney and former solicitor general of the United States. Olson had argued more than sixty cases before the Supreme Court—including the famous *Bush v. Gore* case that decided the presidency in 2000, which is where I first got to know him. In 2009, Olson surprised many conservatives and liberals alike when he took on California's Proposition 8, which rolled back same-sex marriage in the state before the U.S. Supreme Court made marriage equality the law of the land.

Olson explained that lawyers like yes-no questions because they establish the record and draw precise boundaries. They put on the record a definitive response to a specific action or moment and give the questioner almost complete control over the witness and the testimony.

"You basically want to channel the witness into one of these box canyons you used to see in western movies," Olson told me over lunch in downtown D.C. The advantage lawyers have going to trial is that they have studied the evidence and pored over the facts of the case. They have deposed the witnesses and can anticipate what those witnesses will say.

"It is good to ask the questions you already know the answer to—it's very important to do that," Olson says, "and to put [people] in a frame in which you're having a dialogue, getting people somewhat comfortable with the rhythm. And then go someplace that maybe they haven't anticipated."

> *In the article you published on August 13, did you write these*
> *words. . . ?*
> *Did you believe those words when you wrote them?*
> *Do you still believe those words?*

"And the nice thing about yes-no is that the witness puts himself or herself on the record, and they're on the record categorically. What you don't want in trial," Olson advises, "is a lot of open-ended questions, because then the witness has no boundaries and may say something that you don't anticipate and is damaging to your case. You don't want to give the witness an opportunity for an exposition."

Olson observes that a judge may still give the witness an opportunity to explain because "most things in life are not yes or no." But asking yes-no questions conveys a purpose and a strategy.

Yes or no can paint a vivid picture. Oprah Winfrey did not make her name by grilling people. Confrontation and accountability are not her trademarks. But when she sat down with disgraced cycling champion Lance Armstrong for his first interview since he admitted to doping, she launched a series of surgical strike, yes-no questions that categorically established the facts.

OPRAH: *Did you ever take banned substances to enhance your cycling performance?*

ARMSTRONG: *Yes.*

OPRAH: *Was one of those banned substances EPO, which stimulates red blood cell production?*

ARMSTRONG: *Yes.*

OPRAH: *Did you ever blood dope or use blood transfusions to enhance your cycling performance?*

ARMSTRONG: *Yes.*

OPRAH: *Did you ever use any other banned substances such as testosterone, cortisone, or human growth hormone?*

ARMSTRONG: *Yes.*

OPRAH: *In all seven of your Tour de France victories, did you ever take banned substances or blood dope?*

ARMSTRONG: *Yes.*

Having gotten the fallen hero to acknowledge his guilt, Oprah then took him through an extended conversation on his motivations and the consequences of his actions, along with the prevalence of doping in the sport he betrayed.

Armstrong may have hoped the exchange would provide some made-for-television redemption. It did not. But the interview clearly showed how effective yes-or-no, guilt-or-innocence questioning can be when the case is airtight, the prosecutor is disciplined, and the questions are precise and based on information you can bank on.

"It's an art, it's psychology, it's brains, it's communication, and it's theater," Olson counseled. For the record.

Blunt Force

It's not often you get a Lance Armstrong confessing to his sins. Donald Trump certainly didn't recant when Jorge Ramos pressed him. Mary Landrieu wouldn't assign fault, no matter how many times Anderson Cooper asked. I can't think of a single occasion when a politician dropped to his knees after being asked tough questions to say, "Thank you for grilling me like this . . . YES, I am a hypocrite. YES, I lied to the public. OF COURSE, I don't believe half the stuff I say in public."

But we ask these questions to get answers where we can. We use them to make a case, to say, "What you have said or done is not acceptable and you will be held accountable."

Whether you're taking on your boss or your mayor, your mother-in-law (which I don't recommend) or the hapless customer representative at the airline that just left you stranded midway through your journey, your questions matter and make a point.

But you don't want to pick a fight needlessly and you don't want to be wrong. Accountability questions cannot be shots in the dark. They must aim at a real target. When you question and confront, draw from the knowledge you have and set the agenda. Listen closely to control it. If you hear a speech, stop it. If you hear dissembling, call it. If you detect weakness, zero in on it. Where you detect evasion, challenge it. If someone talks in circles or ignores the question, reassert control and ask again.

Confrontational questions entail risk because they put relationships and reputations on the line. Before you confront anyone, ask:

Is confrontation called for?
Are the questions clear and compelling?
Am I willing to stake my reputation on them?

After all, if you're wrong or if you sound ill-informed or like a bully, the questions will boomerang and hit you, not the person you are trying to hold to account.

Ask yourself when and where. Is it appropriate to confront a subordinate in a staff meeting? With others present? Over lunch? Or in a private meeting in the office? Timing, venue, and atmospherics of this type of questioning define the dynamic.

Reflect on exactly how you want to frame your questions. Should they come in a series of short, sharp yes-or-no queries? Or should they be preceded by a recitation of the evidence to frame the issue and establish the premise? Think of tone and whether the questions should be served up with sarcasm or delivered with solemnity, posed in sadness or in anger. The theatrics of confrontational questioning matters, sometimes as much as the answers you get.

Consider the value of the relationship. I didn't really care if I angered Yasser Arafat or if I ever saw him again, though I was keenly aware that my hosts probably did not want him to storm out. Anderson Cooper isn't planning on having lunch with Mary Landrieu, and Donald Trump probably won't be buying Jorge Ramos a vanilla milkshake. If you're going to ask for accountability or confront someone with accusatory questions, consider the cost and be sure you're willing to pay it.

Confrontational questions are the blunt force instruments of inquiry. But they are necessary if we are to live in a place where everyone respects and plays by the rules and is accountable for their actions.

CHAPTER 7

IMAGINE THIS
Creativity Questions

CREATIVITY QUESTIONS INVITE US to pull out the paintbrush, throw away the coloring book and think differently. They prompt our imaginations. They ask us to get out of the way, break rules of convention, and exceed the bounds of the possible. They encourage us to rally to greatness or peer into the future, to see a new world. They invite us to daydream.

What would it be like to ride around like a millionaire?

What a great question. It asks us to envision wealth and comfort replacing the common chore of getting from one place to another. It prods us to imagine how special we'd feel if a deferential driver did the navigating and if convenience replaced stress. No wasted time finding a parking space or hailing a cab. No digging through your pockets for money. (Millionaires don't carry money, anyway.) You stretch out in the back seat, comfortable and relaxed, managing the empire. Absolute efficiency. Pampered success.

It is the question that animated a couple of techie dreamers in a late-night brainstorming session. Travis Kalanick and Garrett Camp were "jamming on ideas, rapping on what's next." Camp came up with a Big

Idea: a solution to the horrible taxi service in San Francisco. Camp was stuck on creating a car service that was so efficient people would feel they were riding like millionaires. In the summer of 2010, the pair launched a tiny company. They called it Uber.

Within four years, Uber reported that riders were taking more than one million trips a day in more than fifty countries. Five years after it started, the company was valued at as much as $50 *billion*. It inspired the "sharing economy," as companies like Airbnb, Snapgoods, and Task-Rabbit remade the way people travel, work, buy, and do business around the world. So now we know. If people are given an opportunity to ride around like a millionaire, they'll do it, millions of times over.

Questions that drive creative thinking are out-there questions. They are big and bold. They ask people to transport themselves to a different time and place and state of mind. They open the door to aspiration and disruption. They challenge the status quo. They reframe issues around visionary, maybe even revolutionary, ideas.

You find inspiration in these fun questions because they invite fresh and original thinking. But you may also feel uneasy when they challenge conventional wisdom and the world you know. Whether you're trying to invent the next big thing, make a crazy video to sell cars, or write the next inspiring chapter in your life, this line of questioning can help you hatch ambitious new ideas and bring people along for the ride to collaborate and create alongside you. Creativity questions ask you to pretend as they connect you to an imagined reality, where horizons are brighter and where limitations are lifted. They are questions that suggest everything is possible.

That's what it's like to ride around like a millionaire.

Creativity questions may not hand you the next $50 billion business, but they will help you put together the best brainstorming session you've ever imagined. They will help you reset the dial and think about new ways to get the kids to be on time or eat their broccoli. They will help you bring divergent viewpoints together and think about new ways to address a problem in the community or in the country. Creative questions can become a collaborative quest for answers.

What's the magic wand idea?
We've arrived. What are we doing?
There are no obstacles. Now what?

Creative questioning asks people to close their eyes and imagine. It welcomes crazy ideas, shrugs off the obvious, and seeks alternatives. Creative questioning asks fellow travelers to:

Set sights unreasonably high. Ask more of yourself and others without being limited by the laws of gravity. There will be plenty of time to come back to earth later. If you don't aim high, you will never go into orbit.

Try a little time travel. Creative thinking is all about the future, so go there. Put your questions in the future tense and ask people to transport themselves there with you.

Invoke imagined reality. Role-play. You're living in that new world, workplace, or community. What's it like? Look up, down, 360 degrees around. What do you see? What do you think? What's next?

Embrace disruption. Questions that drive creativity involve disruptive thinking that can be unsettling, uncomfortable, and sometimes downright subversive. That's how we change the world.

Beyond the Possible

Creativity questions reach for the stars. Which is how we got to the moon.

When Soviet cosmonaut Yuri Gagarin became the first human being to go into space on April 12, 1961, a wave of patriotic pride washed across the Soviet Union—and panic engulfed America. The Soviets were winning the Cold War in space.

President John F. Kennedy consulted the experts and set his sights on the moon. In May, he asked Congress to fund the initiative, noting that the scale of the project was so huge that "it will not be one man going to the moon . . . it will be an entire nation. For all of us must work to put him there." Then he set about selling the idea, asking Americans to be bold, think big to do something that had never been done. Kennedy came into office "asking" the nation to think, not about what the country could do for them but what they could do for their country. Now he wanted them to think outside their planetary constraints. When he spoke at Rice University in September 1962, observing that America had always thought big, he posed a set of questions.

> *But why, some say, the moon?*
> *Why choose this as our goal?*
> *Why climb the highest mountain?*
> *Why, thirty-five years ago, fly the Atlantic?*

We do these things, the young president famously said, not because they are easy, but because they are hard.

The brilliance of Kennedy's questions—which were a hallmark not just of the moon shot but so much of his Camelot presidency—was in their ability to appeal to the country's imagination, greatness, and sense of destiny. They asked Americans to rise to a challenge, to look to the future and to answer a higher calling.

The response was hardly unanimous. The Apollo mission was brave and brilliant, but according to Gallup polls conducted before the landing, it never enjoyed majority public support until the day the lunar module actually touched down on the surface of the moon. But when the time came, one out of every seven people on the planet watched the moon landing on TV. I was a kid at summer camp and listened on a battery-operated transistor radio as Neil Armstrong set foot on lunar soil and took his one step for humanity and read from a plaque on the leg of the Eagle Lander, "Here men from planet Earth first set foot on the moon . . . we came in peace for all mankind." On that magical day, July 20, 1969, we rose to an extraordinary challenge and answered Kennedy's questions in a way that captivated the planet.

Travel in Time

When we ask people to time travel—to fast-forward themselves to another place, another time—we issue a ticket to creative thinking. There are few moments in human history that rival the mission to the moon, but we envision the future every day. It's how we set our sights and articulate ambitious goals.

When I started my term as a trustee for my alma mater, Middlebury College, the president was in the early stages of crafting a ten-year strategic plan. At our fall retreat, a facilitator started with a question that invited us to think creatively about the college's future by going there.

"It is ten years from now," he said, "and the latest college rankings have just come out. This school is at the top of the list. What are we doing?"

He put the future in the present tense. His question was a time machine. Once we stepped inside, the obstacles that often interfere with big ideas—practical considerations like cost, resources, staffing, and economics—fell away. We traveled past them and arrived at our destination, where we were the best. In our very own virtual reality, we looked around and listed the qualities that earned us the top spot. There was a new science center, a new library, more students who brought more diversity, more faculty, and more funding. The future was clear!

Everyone played. Then we worked backward to determine how to make it happen, from program design to funding. Today, the college has a beautiful science center and library. There are more students and more faculty. The school is in the top ranks of liberal arts colleges. We did it. Imagined reality became actual reality.

Since that retreat, I have used this technique many times, asking people to time travel to visit the future and see it for themselves. Imagine. It's five years in the future. Your business has moved from number twelve in the marketplace to number three.

What are you doing?
Who are your customers?

What are you known for?
What are you proudest of?

Ask about the future in the present tense. Once you have articulated it, work to achieve it. There are no guarantees, but you can now ask what it will take to hit your benchmarks, who needs to do what, against what odds, and at what cost. You build a brick at a time. But it's a lot easier when you've seen the place and know where you want to go and why.

Cutting Strings

How can questions convey authorship and drive genuine collaboration? How can they encourage people to take ownership of an idea or a concept and think differently, be original, and strive for the truly creative, maybe even the off-the-wall?

I wanted to explore those questions from a different perspective, far from the high-stakes stuff of space travel, politics, and technology. So I decided to go to where imagination exists for its own sake: Hollywood. Now, when you think of Hollywood, deep thought may not be the first thing that comes to mind. However, it is a place where creativity is an industry, where collaboration is a high-voltage necessity and success is measured in numbers—ratings and revenue.

I called my friend Tom Hoberman—a super-agent lawyer in LA who knew just about everyone—and asked him to connect me with the most creative, most inquisitive person he could think of. In a nanosecond, he recommended Ed Bernero, an insanely creative guy whose unlikely trajectory drove a supersonic career.

Ed is a big man with a big personality. His voice booms and stories spill out of him. He is a show runner, director, writer, and producer. He's been involved with hit shows like *Third Watch*, *Criminal Minds*, and *Crossing Lines*. He mines the talent of everyone around him by shoving them out of their comfort zones and into their stories and their characters. He does it with questions that place writers, actors, and others into the imagined reality of story.

Ed isn't a central-casting kind of Hollywood player. He grew up rough in Chicago, seeing his father beat his mother. As a young kid he called the cops more than once. He saw the police as his protectors. After a stint in the military and jobs working for security firms, he became a Chicago cop himself. He lasted nearly ten years—until he quit to save his soul.

Being the good storyteller he is, Bernero describes the scene when he realized he was in trouble, the protagonist confronting his discovered vulnerability. Ed and his partner were two good cops on patrol in a rough neighborhood. They stopped at the liquor store where they checked in every day and where a big guy I'll call Lee kept them up to speed on what was happening on the streets. Lee sold them cigarettes for a quarter a pack. Cheap cigarettes, street-smart cops, and everyone was happy.

One night, Ed stopped by as usual, only to find a stranger behind the counter.

"Where's Lee?" he asked.

"They killed him this morning," the woman said. "Shot in the face." Ed was stunned. He went back to his patrol car and sat there. His first thought: "Where am I going to get cigarettes for 25 cents a pack?" Then he stopped. Lee was dead, and Ed found himself thinking about cheap cigarettes? He shook his head and looked down as he told me the story. It was the moment he knew he had to get out. "That job is a complete erosion of your humanity."

Ed didn't get out for another five years. But he began writing screenplays in his basement. "Not as a job," he told me, "but as therapy."

One day, a friend was picking up an NBC executive from the airport to speak at Northwestern University. Ed's wife had slipped her one of Ed's scripts and asked her to pass it on to the visiting exec. Within days, Ed got a call. Good stuff, he was told, sit tight. More agents and producers called asking for meetings—invoking some of the biggest names in Hollywood: Steven Bochco, John Wells, David Milch.

Three weeks shy of his tenth anniversary with the Chicago police department Ed Bernero pulled his money out of his home, cashed in his pension, and hauled his family across the country. Within a month, he had his first freelance gig—with super-producer Steven Bochco on the

CBS police drama *Brooklyn South*. Following that, he worked with John Wells on the NBC hit show *Third Watch*. Ed ended up doing more than 130 episodes of New York cop dramas, many of them drawn from his own experience.

But Ed found Hollywood a strange place—riddled with back-lot intrigue, hypersensitive egos, and no shortage of pandering and posturing. Directors, producers, show runners, and studio execs maneuver for recognition and influence. Writers think every word is a gem. Actors take their craft, and themselves, very seriously. Just about everyone is insecure or desperate to get the big break and will say anything to ingratiate them with whoever is calling the shots. Ed once wrote a deliberately terrible script and took it to a crew meeting to see if anyone would call him on it. They didn't. He realized that if he was going to get genuinely creative work out of his team and not just his own ideas thrown back at him, he needed to engage them differently. He couldn't bark orders—he had to ask.

You can't treat people like puppets on a string, Ed told me.

The creativity Ed wants to inspire requires collaboration. "I want everyone to be involved in the show," he said. It starts in the writers' room, where ideas collide in mid-thought and mid-air. The room is dominated by a big table that is bounded by whiteboards and littered with chips and pretzels and energy food. This is where Ed's writers "break the story." They jot down an idea, kick around plot points, story elements, twists and turns, and imagine how the whole thing unfolds.

Ed wants his writers to construct original, bold, surprising stories— to "color outside the lines." But he knows that if he tells writers what he's thinking about a scene or a character, they will be tempted to run with it, play it safe, and give him what they think he wants. So he uses questions to challenge the room.

What if the hero shows up late?
What if the bad guy missed his mark?

The questions are designed to get the writers and the rest of the crew peering around the corner, inventing surprising twists and turns in the story. Ed uses this technique to foster an atmosphere that's edgy, highly charged, and fun. He wants brainstorming and energy. He also wants creative tension. Ed can be a pain in the ass, and he knows it. He will send scripts back to the team with corrections and complaints. He will say something's terrible. He usually eats lunch alone in his office. It's not because he's shy. He wants to give his team their space. "I want them to bitch about me," he told me. "I want them to care enough to be upset. I tell them all, at some point during the season you're going to hate me. That's okay. It's like a family. You can storm out. You can be emotional."

Ed barks questions, not orders, to challenge his writers.

How can you improve the character?
What happens next?

But he also uses questions to make people feel involved and invested. "Otherwise they will just sort of quietly wait for you to say something, and go and do it. It's the same with the crew as it is in a writing room. I can change the whole direction of the story just by saying something." Ed believes he brings out the most creative thinking from people when he asks.

He recalls shooting a scene when an actor playing a cop couldn't nail the timing of a critical move. Squaring off in the street against a woman who is the prime suspect in a criminal investigation, the cop gets his first opportunity to question her. She is crouched and defensive. The cop studies her through his sunglasses, sending signals of authority and accusation. At the right moment, the cop pulls away his sunglasses to make eye contact. After several tries, Ed sees it isn't working.

"Take five!" Ed calls out, approaching his cop-actor to discuss the scene. Ed does not tell him, "On the third line take your sunglasses off. . . ." Instead he asks, "When do you think this character would want to show his eyes? That's the moment the suspect sees into you." Ed wants his actor to think about his eyes, not the glasses. "So when do you want that to happen?"

By turning a direction into a question, Ed handed the responsibility for the answer to his actor, asking *him* to picture the scene and solve the problem. It wasn't just about his lines, it was about the chemistry between two characters that, in turn, shaped the story. The actor had to feel it intuitively. The next take, Ed recalled, was perfect.

"Actors are extremely emotional people and extremely sensitive," Ed explained. "You can't just go in and tell them. You have to find a way to ask and find out what they're thinking and value." Once you do that they help answer the question. Now they can close their eyes and imagine.

Ed could be talking about anyone in any place. If you're trying to devise a new way of approaching a problem, if you're hoping to get the creative juices flowing, your question can be an invitation.

> *How would you do this differently?*
> *What's your new idea?*

These questions are invitations to contribute and create. They send a signal of respect. They offer a challenge that says, "you are a valued part of the expedition. Where to?"

Imagined Reality

Creativity questions have an almost magical capacity to transport people to a different time, place, or perspective. They help us get to that imagined reality. Like Ed Bernero, we can use these questions to craft a story that's original and different.

A publisher friend of mine, Jay, convened an off-site retreat with his top editors. He began with an exercise. Crunch time had arrived and each magazine had to cut its budget by 50 percent. He asked:

> *What do you cut?*
> *What do you do?*
> *Were do you start?*

The teams went to work, prioritizing and calculating, cutting staff and expenses and page counts, looking for savings in paper quality and marketing. They looked at circulation and administrative costs. Though this was just an exercise, everyone played along and took it seriously.

Then came the twist. In a surprise move, Jay gave his editors their money back. Every penny. But he told them to use the budget they'd cut just a few minutes earlier as their new baseline. They could invest the money they had "saved" in any way they wanted.

What will you build?
How will you invest?

Their answers helped transform the company's five newsstand magazines and led to more National Magazine Awards than any of their rivals. The net profit for the company doubled in two years.

Asking people to play a role and answer a series of questions or a challenge catalyzes creative thought and innovation. The consulting firm McKinsey & Company examined the best ways that businesses could use insights from neuroscience to unleash creativity and innovative ideas in their employees. McKinsey cited the work of neuroscientist Gregory Berns from Emory University, who found that creativity requires "bombarding" our brains with things that are new, unfamiliar, and different.

The McKinsey authors stated, "only by forcing our brains to re-categorize information and move beyond our habitual thinking patterns can we begin to imagine truly novel alternatives." They cited a *Harvard Business Review* article in which professors Clayton Christensen, Jeffrey Dyer, and Hal Gregersen list five "discovery" skills for innovators: associating, questioning, observing, experimenting, and networking. They found that making connections across "seemingly unrelated questions, problems, or ideas" was the most effective path to innovation and that analogies—comparing one company to another, just as Kennedy compared Apollo to Lindberg and as the Uber boys created a comparison between a taxi and a millionaire's limousine—led the teams to "make considerable creative progress."

They provided some sample questions that businesses could use in a brainstorming session, asking what the best in the business would do in their shoes, drawing comparisons that most closely applied to their own challenges. After all, *creativity questions* should be aspirational.

> *How would Google manage our data?*
> *How might Disney engage with our consumers?*
> *How could Southwest Airlines cut our costs?*
> *How would Zara redesign our supply chain?*

Pushing people out of their "habitual thinking patterns" is an exercise anyone can do. Imagine that your daughter just won a full-freight scholarship to any school in the world. Ask her:

> *Where would she go?*
> *What would she study?*
> *What opportunities would she have?*

Or imagine you were named CEO of your company.

> *What would be the first things you would do to improve morale and performance?*

Role-playing puts people, like Ed's actors, in an imaginary place and asks them to play their part. The exercise works because, often without realizing it, players combine imagination with intellect and get into the game. They think in a hypothetical space and craft their responses to keep up with a storyline they cannot control or predict.

After the 9/11 terror attacks, I ran an exercise with about two dozen governors from across the country. They sat around a big horseshoe-shaped table. They knew the stakes and they were up for the game. My job was to steer them through the scenario to test response and readiness. I opened with a video "news report" of an attack on a shopping mall. Early reports indicated many casualties. Emergency responders were on the scene, but it was a confusing, chaotic situation. Cable news and local TV channels had scrambled trucks, cameras, and crews. The "experts" speculated. Several of them predicted more attacks. I put the governors in the middle of this situation and asked them to envision the scene and their response.

What was the first call they made?
Who needed to be in the room?
What would they tell the public?

A few minutes into the game, I turned to a governor from a midwestern state. I asked him what he was doing amid the heightened alert. Watching closely, he said, but not much more because his state didn't really have strategic targets and had never considered itself seriously at risk. I was stunned. Did he really think anyone was immune from this scourge?

So I added a few more details. I said I was an editor at the *Wall Street Journal* and I wanted to see how the terror alert was playing in places that were off the beaten track and previously had not faced a serious threat. The assignment: Are they prepared or are they complacent? What are they doing? I'd dispatched one of my best, toughest reporters to his state to do the story, I told the governor. She was waiting outside his office now.

What will you say?
What is your headline?

The governor's expression changed. It was as if someone had told him his fly was down as he stepped away from the podium after a big speech. I could see the wheels turning. Reporters? Publicity? Headlines? Well, he said, he would explain how he had met with his emergency management and law enforcement teams. He was coordinating with the Department of Homeland Security. He was monitoring the situation, urging people to be calm but vigilant. Suddenly we had one very in-charge governor. By asking him to imagine himself in a different, fictional place, I prompted him to think hypothetically—creatively.

Afterward, one of the governor's top emergency management aides took me aside and thanked me, quietly observing that the role-playing questions were just what the governor needed to understand what was at stake, and that such a scenario could actually happen. He needed to imagine reality to appreciate it.

Ask for Subversion

Creative, disruptive thinkers are unafraid to ask questions that push the bounds of the present and the possible. They see the world differently and challenge it profoundly. They ask more of themselves and everyone else. Sometimes they are celebrated, sometimes they are vilified. Which is what drew me to the former mayor of San Francisco. Gavin Newsom, defined by his contradictions and known for his willingness to experiment, posed questions that put him on the front lines of astonishing and controversial social change.

At just thirty-four years old, Newsom was the youngest mayor elected in San Francisco in more than a century. He brought boundless energy, a conspicuous determination to innovate, and one of the most interesting pedigrees of anyone who'd ever occupied the job. He was raised by a single mother who took in foster kids and worked three jobs to make ends meet. Hampered by dyslexia, a disability that required special classes and extra effort, and left him "unbelievably timid and insecure," Newsom developed a different way of looking at the world and a deeper appreciation for the underdog and the outcast. As a kid, Newsom had a rough ride. Students laughed at him when he tried to read out loud. Teachers wrote him up for a lack of engagement and focus. He plowed his way through school, but ended up attending half a dozen different schools in eight years.

Though the family had little, they were lucky that a fortuitous friendship had endured. Newsom's father, Bill, went to school with super-rich Gordon Getty, and they had remained close. Young Gavin became friends with Getty's son. He hung out with the family, flew on their private planes, and joined them on African safaris. The Gettys liked Newsom's originality, his sense of adventure and willingness to take risks. They saw potential. Later, they invested in his businesses, which propelled Newsom to wealth, fame, influence—and City Hall.

Newsom remains a study in contrasts. He advocates for the little guy but he cavorts with high rollers. He loves politics but hates what it has become, too often driven by money, self-interest, and ideology. He knows he must build coalitions, but he insists he's still a risk taker. He takes special pride in a plaque on his desk. It is a question. Everyone who comes into his office sees it.

What would you do if you knew you could not fail?

"I challenge my staff and those around me to ask it," he told me. And he challenges himself with it. His first test, and the controversy that was to define him as a politician, came less than two weeks after he was elected mayor, when he attended President George W. Bush's 2004 State of the Union address.

The galvanizing issue was one that reverberated back in San Francisco— same-sex marriage. The president previously had expressed his fierce opposition to it. He was a staunch supporter of the Defense of Marriage Act, which defined marriage as a strictly heterosexual institution. But in this speech, Bush went further. He said he supported a constitutional amendment enshrining marriage as a union between a man and a woman. The speech disturbed Newsom, but a comment afterward enraged him. As he lined up to leave the chamber, Newsom overheard a woman talking about how proud she was of the president for standing up to "the homosexuals." Newsom left Capitol Hill fuming, thinking it was a good thing that few recognized the new, young mayor from gay-friendly San Francisco.

The first person Newsom called was his chief of staff, Steve Kawa— the first openly gay man to serve in that position. Newsom told him they had to "do something about this." When he got home, Newsom convened his team. He posed the questions he'd been asking himself over and over again since the president's speech.

What is this really about?
What values are at stake?
What was the point of becoming mayor?
What did we come here to do?

By now, Newsom viewed the issue as a fundamental matter of fairness and equity. He was leaning in favor of unilaterally instructing City Hall to issue marriage licenses to same-sex couples. Initially even his gay chief-of-staff was opposed. "He fought me," Newsom explained. "He was emotional about it." Kawa saw huge political risks; he knew that it would put everyone in the spotlight and stir up more controversy, even in San Francisco.

"He said it was hard enough to come out to his family," Newsom recalled. But the mayor decided gay people had a right to get married if they wished.

When City Hall opened for business on February 12, 2004—just three weeks after Bush's State of the Union speech—gay couples could apply for marriage licenses for the first time ever. Thousands showed up. Sure enough, Newsom's act of defiance drew the wrath of Republicans and Democrats alike.

"My party leadership was furious and read me the riot act," he said. California senator Dianne Feinstein all but accused the young mayor of sowing the seeds for the Democrats' defeat in the fall's presidential election. Newsom wasn't sure he would survive the storm, but he held his ground. Defending himself on CNN, he said that denying the right to marry "is wrong and inconsistent with the values this country holds dear." He added, "And if that means my political career ends, so be it."

His career did not end. On the contrary, he won reelection with 72 percent of the vote in 2007. He is now lieutenant governor of California with aspirations for higher office. In the decade since San Francisco City Hall issued its first marriage license to same-sex couples, judges, legislatures, and, in 2015, the Supreme Court voted to legalize same-sex marriage. Whatever you may think of Newsom, his role as a change agent on this issue can be traced to those questions he asked himself after hearing a speech. They forced him to step back from the noise and the risks and look at the issue differently. They led him to think differently and defiantly about a once-unimaginable future. Simple questions.

What is this about?
What are our values?
What was I elected to do?

Creative questions ask you to close your eyes and imagine. They are aspirational, often inspiring, and sometimes subversive. They embrace risk and challenge our brains to look through a different lens. While they can be adventurous, even exhilarating, they can also be lonely and controversial.

You can ask these questions of your inventive colleagues or your reluctant stakeholders. You can pose them as a game or as a challenge. You can frame them around the future as you ask for new ways of thinking and doing that will get you there. Creativity questions are daring, liberating queries that invite you to stick your head in the clouds, ask more of everyone, and imagine just how far you can go.

What would you do if you knew you could not fail?

CHAPTER 8

THE SOLVABLE PROBLEM

Mission Questions

HOW CAN YOU USE the power of questions to build a team, clarify your mission, and define your goals? How do you ask people to join you in partnership to make a difference in the world or in your work? You may be trying to raise money for a cause or organize a neighborhood activity, looking into a mentoring program at the office to work with at-risk students, or launching a social media campaign to mobilize people to combat global warming. Perhaps you need to invigorate your team to compete with the new business in town that has hired a bunch of young hotshots.

Mission questions ask more of everybody. They help you draw people into a genuine conversation about shared goals and what everyone can bring to the task. They help you convey your priorities. Mission questions require you to talk less and listen more.

In this chapter you'll see how you can connect people to purpose and forge a common mission. You will learn how to ask questions that can take you from conversation to collaboration. My friend does it to feed the world. One of the most iconic brands did it and turned shared values into a recipe for success that built a legion of loyal employees and customers. A leader in philanthropy draws from pages of great questions to nurture relationships and raise millions of dollars.

Get good at these mission questions and you will be able to do more than build a team. You will inspire it as you help people discover their purpose, find a role they can play, and collaborate to get things done. In asking people to sign on and pitch in you're asking them to:

Identify your mission. Determine interests and see where experiences intersect. What do you care about? What would you like to change or fix or build?

Share values. Find out if you're rowing to the same place. What are your bedrock principles? Where is your true north? How can we partner?

Play a role. Figure out what each party adds to the equation. What are others prepared to do about the problem? What's their expertise, their passion, their capability?

Aim high. People are excited by big ideas. How bold can we be? How will we change the world?

Whether you're raising money for a university or trying to get your kids to participate in a local charity, asking people to commit time, energy, or money to a cause is a big deal. They have to care about your endeavor and want to be a part of it. They have to believe in you and in your objectives. So, ask about values and priorities. Find out what resonates and where your common interests lie. The answers may lead to collaboration and commitment.

Listening for Common Goals

Ed Scott and I met in New York in 2012, when I was speaking about the sorry state of American politics. Pretty bad, I said. Polarized, paralyzed, nasty. And the media? They're not helping. Happy to swarm a controversy or scandal, slow to cover solutions or compromise, the media bring a 24/7 microscope to the bacteria of politics. The public bears responsibility, too, I said. Voters should do their homework so they can separate what's real from what's noise. They need to hold politicians, the media, and themselves to account.

After my talk, Ed said he had some ideas he wanted to discuss. We scheduled a meeting a few weeks later in my office. As I prepared for our meeting, I learned that Ed cared about a lot of things—public health, HIV/AIDS, autism, education, civic engagement. I learned that he'd made a bunch of money in technology and since getting out, he'd quietly invested in causes as well as businesses. He helped start the Center for Global Development; Friends of the Global Fight Against AIDS, Tuberculosis, and Malaria; the Scott Center for Autism Treatment at the Florida Institute of Technology; and the Scott Family Liberia Fellows Program.

We met on campus in the modest conference room down the hall from my office. Ed talked about his exasperation with the political process, his frustration with the media, his concern that the public was ill-informed, and his determination to do something about it. I wanted to understand what he was thinking.

What worries you the most?

Politicians getting off with vacuous ideas and ridiculous sound bites that drown out serious debate about real problems.

Where does the problem lie?

In endless campaigns, fueled by bottomless bank accounts, blind ideology, and scattershot media.

What are the consequences?

People have more opinions than facts. We need to get better information out there—verifiable, impeccable, nonpartisan information. Facts, not opinions about where and how America spends money on foreign aid, education, infrastructure, jobs, climate change, and more. People should have information about jobs and the global economy and trade. That way, Ed felt, maybe we'd have a country where politics and big decisions would more closely correlate to reality.

What could we do about it?

After hours of brainstorming, we came up with an idea. Ed would provide financing and build a board of advisers for "Face the Facts USA." It brought together undergraduate and graduate students and professional journalists to produce a website, videos, infographics, TV specials, and live events built on original, deeply researched facts—100 facts in the 100 days leading up to the 2012 election. It was an ambitious idea with a preposterously short runway.

We developed and launched our fact-a-day project in just three months. We gave away our daily facts to news organizations, talk shows, and civic groups. We used social media to build audience. While our project did not change the world or transform politics, we showed that it was possible to drive conversation built on undisputed and straightforward facts.

Ed and I had discovered our common goals by asking one another about the challenges the country faced and listening closely to each other as we kicked around ideas about what should be done and what each of us could contribute. Ed is a man of conscience and clear vision. Collaborating with him was richly rewarding.

"I try to fix things I care about," Ed said, "driven by values and mission."

The Value Proposition

Asking about goals and interests—and listening closely for the answers—drives Karen Osborne. Karen started the Osborne Group to provide advice and instruction on fundraising for schools and nonprofits that depend on philanthropy and has raised money for hospitals, schools, research organizations, civic groups, and cities. She draws from pages of questions she has composed to create a customized discussion. Like a menu at a restaurant, she offers starter questions to get you going, then main courses to chew on and desserts to end on a high note. I met her through a colleague who had heard Osborne speak and was impressed with her insight on the power of questions to establish shared mission and meaningful associations.

Osborne grew up in the South Bronx. Her family had emigrated from the West Indies. Her father, a manager with the Social Security Administration, was about the only person she knew with a white-collar job. The neighbors in the duplexes around them—African Americans, Italians, and Jews—were mostly firemen, cops, transit workers, and teachers. Surrounded by diversity long before it was celebrated, Osborne was captivated by the people around her, each a compelling character, each in search of some form of the American Dream. A voracious reader, young Karen devoured five or six books a week. She loved getting lost in her reading, getting to know the characters and their adventures, imagining the places the books took her.

In college, Osborne majored in English literature, hoping to be a writer. But she didn't have the luxury of spending years in the attic hoping to hit on the great American novel. So, after college, she got a job in Tarrytown, New York, helping to figure out how to access state and federal funding. She got good at it. She started working with universities, hospitals, and other nonprofits that needed to raise money.

When she set up her own consulting company, Osborne developed a set of questions to help her identify what people care about and where and why they give. She asked about their work, life passions, goals, and objectives. If they had a track record of giving philanthropically, she wanted to know where that came from, what it connected to.

What values underpin your philanthropic decision making?

Osborne's *discovery questions* generate a conversation. They ask what people care about and the motivations behind their passion. Perhaps someone lost a relative to cancer or was moved by an experience with at-risk youth. If they are now in a position to do something more about the problem, what will they do?

"In a discovery visit, I'm trying to learn enough about you so I can craft a strategy that I can develop for you to have a joyful experience," she says.

How do you like being engaged?
How do we fit?

Osborne's "rapport building" questions define principles and goals and connect past actions with future aspirations. They establish a conversation and build a relationship.

What are the guiding principles that have helped you in life?
What do you hope to accomplish with your philanthropy?
What values do you consistently support?

Osborne asks her questions to get answers, but she also asks to be sure the other person is doing the talking. She explained to me that her experience bears out the research: "People forget what they heard, but they remember almost everything they say."

Imagine you're trying to raise money for a new pediatric cancer wing at the local hospital and you're looking for community leaders to sign on to help. You take James out for lunch to see if he will join the cause. You can talk for twenty minutes and explain the new wing, what it will do, why it is needed, who else is supporting it, or you can ask James about the initiative.

What have you heard about the project?
How familiar are you with what the new wing will allow us
to do?
What do you think it will mean for the community?

If James says, "This could make a huge difference for these kids," or talks about what he's read or heard about the project, or if he reflects on a friend who had a child with cancer, he will have joined the conversation more personally than if he just sat and listened. Your questions prompt him to answer and to engage. That's a critical step, Osborne says, if people are going to embrace a cause for which they're going to provide significant financial support.

Want to get people to turn out for your class reunion *and* give money? Get them talking about what they did the last day at school or about the all-nighter they pulled when they were working on the hardest paper of their lives. Ask them about their favorite home game or their best friend. Invite them to tell stories about what the place meant to them and the difference it made. Then connect it back to the fundamentals.

How did you use the education you got from this institution?
What values did you learn?
Are there ways you would like to help the next generation
   of students?

Your questions move to the next level: how can you work together? They seek genuine engagement, and Osborne insists that engagement is the key to philanthropy. She cited a Bank of America study of wealthy people who were philanthropic. The more they were involved in an initiative, the more they gave to it. If their children were involved, they gave even more.

Connect passion to mission and you can generate excitement and meaningful involvement.

"Now I'm excited about the outcome and I start seeing myself as a donor," Osborne instructed me. "And [it's] not just my money, but my interests, my intellectual capital, my human capital, my network capital, and how I might leverage all of those things to help solve this problem together with you, in partnership with you. We're asking for so much more than money." You have defined and are pursuing a common goal.

Change the World

Once you have established the mission and concluded that your goals coincide, you can start thinking about the next step: actually doing something.

What will your partnership look like?
How far will you reach?
Who will do what?
What can you accomplish?

My friend Rick Leach has asked these questions his entire career, dealing with some of the most difficult challenges in the world. He helped lead child immunization efforts, antismoking campaigns, and programs to crack down on counterfeit drug trafficking. In 1997, he started the World Food Program USA, which supports the global World Food Program, the world's largest humanitarian program to combat hunger.

The organization's goal would make Karen Osborne proud for its boldness, clarity, and big question.

Imagine a world without hunger . . . what would it take?

Leach rallies support, raises money, and finds partners in business and government to support efforts to get desperately needed food to victims of drought, poverty, war, and natural disaster. For such a daunting and urgent job—there are more than 700 million people who face food insecurity in the world, including more than 60 million people displaced by war—Leach is one of the most optimistic guys I've ever met. He often greets friends with a loud, "Sweetheart!" from half a room away. He wears a steady smile under his thick mustache. He believes passionately in humanity's capacity for good even though he has stared into its darkest, most desolate places.

Leach has rallied some of the biggest companies, government agencies, NGOs, and hundreds of thousands of citizens to his cause. To attract people to social movements, he believes, you must engage their curiosity and connect passion with mission. He focuses on turning commitment into concrete action. "It's about earnestly asking questions and learning to more fully hone the need in search of the opportunity to address the need," he told me. Leach is an organizer.

His template for partnerships is built on four questions.

How do we define the problem?
What are the strategies to solving the problem?
What's the goal?
How can we all play a role in achieving the goal?

Leach is especially interested in answers to that last question. That's how he and his team know whom to ask for money, time, logistics, and support when a crisis erupts.

"It all gets back to 'What's the problem?'" Leach explained. "What do we need to do to address it? What's your role?"

He offers the 2015 Ebola crisis as an example. When Ebola hit, food and nutrition quickly became one of the big problems as whole areas of some countries shut down. Business stopped. Leach turned to his long-time sponsor, UPS, knowing its capacity in logistics. With staging areas around the world, the company delivers 18 million packages every day. Leach asked if UPS would help distribute food, medical supplies, generators, and equipment. UPS agreed. The company provided invaluable logistical support, using its Cologne-based facility to assemble material, equipment, and relief supplies and fly them into West Africa for use by the humanitarian community. World Food Program distributed food to more than 3 million people in the year and a half after the Ebola outbreak.

Leach's approach to mobilizing people and defining roles can be applied at virtually any level—whether you are trying to change the world or the town where you live. You may want to organize your friends at work and launch a high school mentoring program or engage your neighbors to give up a few weekends and clean the riverfront. Maybe you'd like to raise money for the agency that provides housing for the disabled. Get good people together and use Leach's questions to define the challenge, consider strategies, and set roles.

Thousands of ordinary people—25,786 to be exact—contributed to his organization in 2015. Commitment like that is what inspires him to go to work each day and maintain his optimism.

"Hunger is a solvable problem," he says in his completely confident way. "We can do this."

Sharing Works

Discovering shared purpose can be about changing the world. Or it can be about changing your life and partnering with someone who shares your sense of adventure.

For Ben Cohen and Jerry Greenfield, finding their shared values was easy; figuring out how to act on them was the harder part.

What would we really like to do?

Their story is well known. They met in seventh-grade gym class, where, by their own admission, they were the "slowest, fattest kids in the class." In high school they became best buds. Jerry attended Oberlin College. Ben started out at Colgate, before dropping out. Jerry thought about medical school but went into pottery. Both liked to eat. They considered going into the bagel business but the equipment cost far more than they had, which was just about nothing. So they decided to make ice cream. And with that, Ben & Jerry's was born.

With only a $5 correspondence course in ice cream making under their belts, they weren't exactly in line for the Forbes 100. What they *did* have, however, were deeply shared values and goals. Pretty simple ones. In their book, *Ben & Jerry's Double-Dip*, they wrote, "We wanted to have fun, we wanted to earn a living, and we wanted to give something back to the community."

What values do we bring to the enterprise?

They opened their first store in Shelburne, Vermont, in 1978. By 1990 they had grown into an iconic brand known for quality products and a distinctive voice. They built the company around values. They sought ideas from employees through companywide surveys. They asked about the product, the workplace, and their causes.

How do we incorporate values into our work and activities?

Ben and Jerry translated their values into public actions. They launched a foundation to support community causes and devised a compensation model that initially capped the bosses' pay at no more than five times the lowest employees' pay. They championed a string of public causes, emblazoned on every pint of ice cream: 1% for Peace (1988); Take a Stand for Children (1992); Rock the Vote (2004); GMO? Thanks, but NO (2013), to name a few. Though the company has changed since Ben and Jerry actually owned and ran the place, it has retained a good bit of its DNA. The company still asks its employees those survey questions.

If you want to launch an enterprise, go into partnership, or start a values-driven business, ask mission questions to test commitment and direction.

How does the idea reflect your values?
Will others find this worthy?
What's the bumper sticker higher calling?
Can you define roles and will people want to fill them?

Maybe you'll discover the next Cherry Garcia.

What Brings You Here?

At the upscale end of the corporate spectrum, questions are effective tools in defining purpose and motivating mission. I learned how powerful they could be from Diana Oreck, who was working for Ritz-Carlton at the time we met. She explained how the company uses questions to imbue its employees with its "gold standard" ethic.

We ran into one another on one of those packed flights that prompts commiseration among strangers about survival instincts and contortionist skills. Our conversation in "economy class" turned out to be supremely ironic since Oreck is a first-class connoisseur. She hails from the famous family that made a fortune in vacuum cleaners. Growing up in Mexico, she often traveled with her parents as they tended the business. They frequented fine hotels and young Diana fell in love with the glamour and mystique of the fanciest, most exotic places they stayed— the ones with ornate lobbies and mysterious people from around the world. If they stayed long enough, she found that staff became family. The adventure was thrilling. She went into the hotel business, leaving vacuums to the relatives.

Ritz-Carlton owns more than eighty hotels in twenty-six countries. With revenue of more $3 billion a year, the hotels employ 38,000 people. Their goal is to dominate the luxury hospitality business and create genuine brand loyalty in their well-heeled customers. In this super-competitive world, Oreck told me, visitors expect service that goes above and beyond.

"If you have a satisfied customer, you've only met their needs. In this environment that's not enough. You need to exceed expectations." The customer can't be just a transaction and a "head in a bed." There has to be something more.

Oreck trained Ritz-Carlton managers and staff to understand and share the mission so they could fulfill it. Committed to "unique and memorable" experiences that will turn guests into "customers for life," the company wants to create an experience that "enlivens the senses, instills well-being, and fulfills even the unexpressed wishes and needs of our guests."

What defines us?
What do we stand for?
How do we deliver on the promise?

At staff meetings and other gatherings, employees are asked about their ideas and suggestions, their successes and failures. They're encouraged to tell stories—the good, the bad, and the unbelievable. They act out hypothetical scenarios to see if they're living up to the credo that's been drilled into them. A young couple comes to the restaurant with a toddler. What is the first thing you say, the first thing you do? An older couple arrives at check-in and the woman appears stressed and angry. What do you say?

Oreck calls it "radar on, antenna up," driven by good questions, careful listening, and thorough training. She explained that every employee who dealt with guests had authority to unilaterally spend, credit, or discount up to $2,000 per day to "make it right or delight." If you're going to build a workforce that buys into the culture, she explained, you have to empower and engage your employees.

"As an employee, if I have to run to the manager every time I want to help a guest, the company is telling me I'm too stupid to help, or I'm going to give too much away, or you as the company were joking when you said you trusted me."

Ritz-Carlton's training teaches employees to use their own questions to create relationships with the guests and deliver on the mission. A guest goes up to the concierge and asks where the gift shop is. Rather than simply directing the customer down the hall, the concierge will, when possible, accompany the guest partway and may ask, "What brings you to our lovely city?" If the guest says she's in town for a wine tasting, the concierge can use the information to recommend a restaurant with an amazing wine cellar.

Questions don't win the war if they're not accompanied by active and effective listening. "We have a ratio: two ears and one mouth," Oreck notes, telling me that the hotel staff must make "emotional connections." She counsels everyone she trains to listen hard for emotional indicators—joy, anger, frustration. Her lesson plan is mission-focused: Create that experience that will lead to a "customer for life."

Ritz-Carlton is no charity. It is big business. But like Ben & Jerry's and the World Food Program USA, it cannot succeed with its gold-plated mission if the people who work there aren't asked to be part of it and execute it.

Asking to Listen

Throughout this book I've connected the discipline of asking to the art of listening—deep and active listening. In the case of mission questions that seek shared purpose, you're listening for comments and clues that reveal motivations, ambitions, and capacity that align with your mission. If you're asking Jordan to support your cause, you're listening for indications of his commitment and passion. You're listening for comments that show optimism or outrage, inspiration or indignation, or some expression to suggest that Jordan agrees that yours is a worthy cause and he is interested in doing something to advance it.

If you're talking to Clara about financing a business, you will be listening closely for anything she says about the viability of the idea, about the marketplace or the business plan, or about the competition or cash flow. You're listening for hidden or unexpected places to explore and connect. If you hear a suggestion about the satisfaction that comes from giving, you have another topic to ask about:

What have you supported that has really made a difference?

"Oh, that's easy," Clara might say, "It was the work we did on the home for sick kids. We saw the wonderful place get built. It helped entire families get through their ordeal."

How did you get involved in that?

"We met with this amazing woman who so impressed us with her commitment and her approach. We knew that she could pull it off."

Here's where the close listening comes in, and an echo question.

We?

"Yes," comes the reply. "My husband and our daughter, Emma. We make these decisions as a team."

You've just learned essential information about why the family gives, what made for a credible project, and, importantly, *how* they give as a family. You build the relationship accordingly.

Karen Osborne counsels that we can all be better listeners. First, consider what type of listener you are.

> *Do you listen for data, facts, and specifics?*
> *Do you key into stories because you relate to* people*?*
> *Do you respond to emotion?*
> *What interests you and gets your attention?*
> *What prompts you to respond?*
> *How hard is it to remain silent?*

Figuring out what kind of listener you are will help you listen better and craft more precise questions and areas for follow up.

Next, identify your weaknesses.

> *Are you an interrupter?*
> *Are you someone who has to drive a conversation; who has to fill*
> *   silences and pauses?*
> *Does your mind wander?*
> *Do you look down and do email?*
> *Is it because you have trouble focusing or are just bored?*
> *Can you identify the types of conversations or the points along the*
> *   way when your mind might wander?*
> *Do you suffer from the "I syndrome," a habit of instantly turning*
> *   what you just heard into a comment about or reference to*
> *   yourself?*

If you listen closely to yourself and to others, you will discover how many people fall into the "I syndrome" trap and how often it occurs.

Eva is chatting with Tom, who tells her about a minor car accident he was in yesterday. Eva says, "Yeah, I had a fender bender just like that last year . . ."

John is talking to a colleague at work who is worried her higher insurance premiums are going to eat up this year's raise. John says, "Same thing happened to me last year . . ."

You're talking to that potential donor again, who says the best place in a hospital is the maternity ward. You say, "Yes! When my wife had our son . . ."

Stop! Stay focused on your *listening* and *asking*. Keep your questions like your eyes, locked on that other person, on the project you're discussing, and on the *shared* goals. Mission questions demand selfless listening. Talk about *we*, not *I*. Ask more, speak less. This conversation is about common goals, not what you think or what you have done. Understand the connection between the question and the listening. General Colin Powell has a 30 percent rule: When you're running a meeting, speak 30 percent of the time; that forces you to listen 70 percent of the time.

"Questions actually help you listen better," Karen Osborne says. "They help you focus."

And the golden rule in listening is to listen to others as you would want others to listen to you. Be genuinely interested in the other person and what the person has to say. Find the facets of that person's story that are significant or surprising or remarkable to you. Know what they've accomplished or been up against. Be familiar with what makes them special and unique.

Now you're exploring common goals and shared purpose with someone you care about.

Solve Problems with Purpose

Recently, I interviewed a panel of experts who work with the disabled. My job was to ask them about the challenges they faced in connection with a new law about employment for people with disabilities. The discussion centered on the new rules, but my hosts didn't want it to get lost in the weeds of process and bureaucracy. So we focused on the calling, and how to work most effectively with the 38 million Americans who have a disability. I found Rick Leach's organizing questions a useful outline for the conversation.

What is the challenge?
What can you do about it?
What can each of you bring to the enterprise?
What will it take?

In your work and volunteer activities, you can define mission and rally people by asking them first to think about what matters and then where your interests overlap. Ask how they want to participate and engage. Ask them to aim high. That's what Rick Leach does when he asks people to join his campaign to end global hunger. It's why he believes hunger is a "solvable problem."

CHAPTER 9

INTO THE UNKNOWN
Scientific Questions

WE LIVE IN AN AGE of instant answers. I googled this question: *How do we know the earth is round?* In less than one second, I had 168 million results at my fingertips. If I spent one minute on each, it would take me 320 years to get through them all.

We live in an age of assertion. I can fire off a tweet or post an opinion, no matter how accurate or incendiary, and get the attention of the crowd, maybe even go viral. Politicians throw out untruths or half-truths and, even when proven wrong, they will double down and assert again. In 2015, Representative Lamar Smith, chairman of the House Committee on Science, Space, and Technology, declared authoritatively that climate data clearly showed "no warming" for the past two decades. He didn't back down even though 14 of the 15 years from 2000-2015 logged in as the hottest on record, according to data from NASA. Truth is often eclipsed by attitude.

Instant answers and easy assertion populate our digital information age. I can surround myself with friends and associates, virtual or real, who will be my echo chamber, ratifying my ideas and validating my logic. I can live in a media universe where everyone will agree with me, and my social media tribe will cement my certainty.

How do we slow it down?
Can we allow ourselves to be wrong?
Can we ask in a different way?

Up to now, my quest to understand how we ask more of ourselves and one another had taken me through several lines of inquiry, each connected to its own distinct outcome, each calling for its own unique approach. In all of them, the artful question leads to information and awareness, understanding and answers.

But there's a line of inquiry characterized by the slow question, the one that doesn't yield an immediate answer and dares you to embrace uncertainty. I wondered, can the slow question, the kind that requires painstaking work and enduring patience, where you try to prove yourself wrong in order to see if you might be right, be a viable alternative in our world of instant answers? Can it prove to be a reliable path to truth?

The answer, of course, is yes. The slow question exists with a distinctly different approach. It is expressed through the inquisitive lens of science, which ventures into the unknown, seeking to explain the mysteries of the physical world. This questioning method represents a way of asking that recognizes the vastness and uncertainties of the unexplored. The method builds logically from the ground up.

Observe a problem, frame a question. Take what you see or know to be objectively and measurably true from the real world and ask a question. What's going on here? What's causing this?

Offer an explanation. Based on your observations, your experiences, and the facts and data that exist, put together a clear hypothesis that could explain the situation.

Put your hypothesis to the test. Experiment and measure over time. Try to prove yourself wrong. What else could explain this situation? What did you miss? What could be wrong with your approach and your data? If your hypothesis holds up, you are making progress.

Share. If you think you're onto something, shop it around and show it to other knowledgeable people. Let them review it. Do they see something that you didn't? Do they have any problem with your data or your methods? If not, you might just have a theory you can act on.

Scientific questioning drives a process that revolves around data, experimentation, and observable fact. It is a method that tackles a daunting quest and challenges attention spans in an instant-answer world. The discipline this line of questioning imposes makes for better inquiry and better decisions across the board. Think back to a choice you made or an action you took that didn't turn out the way you hoped. Ever wonder how different things would have been if you had more information or looked at what you did have a bit more skeptically? Have you ever worked off an untested instinct or an unchallenged belief and then wished—knowing what you know now—that you could do it all over again, or that you could have road-tested your hunch before you acted on it? How would things have been different if you could have been more scientific in selecting the car you bought or the business you invested in? What if you could turn your search for answers into a science?

The Doctor's Quest

I wondered: Can we inject a little scientific method into the questions we confront every day? How can scientific questioning be useful to the rest of us? First, I had to see how it works. I went to the sprawling campus of the National Institutes of Health (NIH) just outside Washington, D.C., to speak with one of the country's leading scientists. He's worked all his life trying to figure out the unknown, in a world where research is subject to criticism, hypotheses exist to be disproved, and answers lead to more questions.

The world of science in Bethesda, Maryland, stands in jolting contrast to the political world of Washington just down the road, where people expect questions to be answered quickly and decisively. But unlike the political world, science celebrates discovery and the unknown represents a challenge, not a weakness. In science, facts are things to be learned, not exploited. Data, not opinion, holds sway.

Dr. Anthony Fauci has led the National Institute of Allergy and Infectious Diseases for more than three decades. In a town where everyone picks sides, Fauci has mostly stayed out of politics. He sees himself as "an honest broker of science." He gives little credence to political labels and has no patience for ideology that obscures discovery or stands in the way of cures. Fauci deals with medical fact and the painstaking, meticulous research of biological science. His questions grow out of his observations and insatiable thirst for research and for cures to disease.

Fauci greeted me outside his spacious office a few minutes after 7 a.m. This wasn't his first piece of business for the day; he'd been at his desk since 6. He had a reputation as a workaholic, a nonstop guy. A small, super-fit man in his seventies who never lost his Brooklyn accent, Fauci still ran and worked marathon days. His suite of offices was crammed with books and journals and offered a gallery of his life. Pictures with patients, presidents, doctors, and researchers from around the world hung from the walls. They highlight Fauci's work against killer diseases: HIV/AIDS, SARS, malaria, Ebola, and the Zika virus.

Fauci was especially proud of one picture. Taken around 1989, it shows him with President George H. W. Bush and his wife, Barbara, sitting in a crowded semicircle with researchers and AIDS patients. President Bush had just approved a large increase in AIDS funding that Fauci had sought. It was a sharp turn from Bush's predecessor, Ronald Reagan. The funding opened a research pipeline that led to effective treatments for HIV/AIDS and brought dramatic and desperately needed breakthroughs. They came, however, only after years of suffering, controversy, and research.

A Mystery Killer

I first encountered Fauci in the early 1980s when he briefed on a mysterious ailment that seemed to be targeting gay men. The disease didn't even have a name yet. I was covering the White House, where President Reagan was reluctant even to talk about it. He and his wife, Nancy, had plenty of gay friends from their days in California. The actor Rock Hudson, the first major celebrity to die of the disease, had attended a state dinner hosted by the Reagans just three weeks before he was diagnosed. But the ailment, with its implications of homosexuality, was a taboo subject in politics at the time.

Fauci had always been a questioner, an explorer. Like other scientists and researchers, he would see a problem—a disease or an illness—become fascinated by it, and turn it into a research question, derived in some fashion from the most fundamental question in the universe:

What's going on here?

The autoimmune system had been Fauci's specialty in medical school. Trained in immunology and infectious disease, he was absorbed by the question of why the human immune system sometimes turned on itself, robbing the body of its ability to fight off illness and infection. In his early work as a young researcher at NIH, Fauci had been researching an autoimmune disorder known as Wegener's granulomatosis. The disease inflames the blood vessels in the lungs, kidneys, and upper airway. Symptoms include nosebleeds, sinus pain, coughing up blood, skin sores, and fever.

In a laboratory two floors above him, cancer researchers were conducting groundbreaking research into Hodgkin's disease. Fauci regularly ran into his colleagues in the hallways or over a meal. They compared notes, shared observations, and told stories as doctors do. One thing his colleagues told him in particular caught his attention. It seemed cancer patients were prone to infectious diseases as a result of their chemotherapy. The chemo not only suppressed the cancerous tumors, but also the patients' own immune systems. So Fauci wondered:

Could you turn off the immune system without killing the patient in order to cure a disease?

Fauci hypothesized that a delicate balance of low-dose, anticancer drugs could suppress the immune system in Wegener's patients. He knew Wegener's had no cure; treatments had so far been ineffective. Doctors had tried corticoid steroids and prednisone, but patients remained dangerously prone to bacterial infection or the flu.

To test his hypothesis, Fauci's research team began experimenting with low levels of chemo drugs in control groups. They conducted clinical trials and pitted the new drugs against placebos. They tracked their patients over months and kept meticulous records about their health, age, condition, and progress.

"To my incredible gratification and I think a little luck," Fauci told me, "it turned out that the drugs that we picked were just right." The drugs also proved effective for other autoimmune diseases, and Fauci quickly made a name for himself. He appeared to be on track for an extraordinary career in the field of immunology. Then something unforeseen happened that changed Fauci's life.

It began in his office on a Saturday morning early in June 1981. Fauci was scanning the *Morbidity and Mortality Weekly Report*, put out by the Centers for Disease Control (CDC). He read an item about five gay men in Los Angeles who had died as a result of a pneumocystis pneumonia. Caused by a fungus commonly found in the lungs of healthy people, this form of pneumonia can become deadly in those with weakened immune systems. Fauci did a double take and asked himself:

What is going on?
Why all gay men?
Why pneumocystis pneumonia in otherwise healthy gay men?

At first, Fauci thought recreational drugs might be the problem. That wasn't his field of expertise, however, and he was busy with Wegener's research. "What the hell," he figured. "Forget it."

A month later, another CDC morbidity report hit Fauci's desk. It featured another alert about the same mysterious illness. Now it reported that twenty-six men had died, and not just in Los Angeles. Victims were in New York City and San Francisco as well. All were gay. All had seemed in perfect health before coming down with deadly pneumonia. Fauci was alarmed.

"This is going to be huge," he said to himself.

Cultures Clash

Science, medicine, and experience drove Fauci to conclude that we were on the verge of a full-blown health crisis, a new and frighteningly unpredictable illness whose dimensions were completely unknown. He responded as a scientist and as a doctor, thinking in terms of public health. He had been trained to observe a problem and ask about it in a methodical way, putting impulse and judgment to the side.

Outside the gates of science and the NIH, however, there was an altogether different response. I was the White House correspondent for Associated Press Radio. I had recently returned from London, where I'd been based as a foreign correspondent. Now I was assigned to a noisy, cramped, show-offy place where reporters strutted their stuff to show how tough or influential they were, and the press secretary played power politics, leaking stories to those he liked and freezing out those he thought were unfair, unfriendly, or overly hostile. Welcome to the White House Briefing Room. We were just a few miles from NIH but we were in another universe.

On this day, in October 1982, someone in the press corps asked about this new and deadly illness that few others wanted to talk about. The reporter, Lester Kinsolving, was with WorldNetDaily, a conservative news organization committed to "exposing wrongdoing, corruption, and abuse of power." His questions to Reagan's press secretary, Larry Speakes, produced a surreal moment.

> KINSOLVING: *Larry, does the president have any reaction to the announcement {by} the Centers for Disease Control in Atlanta, that AIDS is now an epidemic {in} over 600 cases?*
>
> SPEAKES: *What's AIDS?*
>
> KINSOLVING: *Over a third of them have died. It's known as "gay plague."* (Laughter.) *No, it is. I mean it's a pretty serious thing that one in every three people that gets this has died. And I wondered if the president is aware of it?*
>
> SPEAKES: *I don't have it. Do you?* (Laughter.)
>
> KINSOLVING: *No, I don't.*
>
> SPEAKES: *You didn't answer my question.*
>
> KINSOLVING: *Well, I just wondered, does the president—*
>
> SPEAKES: *How do you know?* (Laughter.)
>
> KINSOLVING: *In other words, the White House looks on this as a great joke?*
>
> SPEAKES: *No, I don't know anything about it, Lester.*
>
> KINSOLVING: *Does the president, does anybody in the White House know about this epidemic, Larry?*
>
> SPEAKES: *I don't think so. I don't think there's been any—*
>
> KINSOLVING: *Nobody knows?*
>
> SPEAKES: *There has been no personal experience here.*

In retrospect and with full knowledge about the suffering to come, the words and laughter from that White House "briefing" ring especially cruel. The exchange revealed ignorance, fear, and the disconnect between politics and science. A deadly disease appeared to be striking young gay men. Did the president have a reaction? No, the press secretary replied, implying: *None of us around here are gay enough to have had that experience.* Speakes made no comment about the health dimension or the research that was needed to solve the crisis. He made no reference to public health or education. He addressed the questions through his peculiar political filter.

It's impossible to look back on this exchange and not find it appalling. But a variation of it happens with alarming frequency. We often respond emotionally or dismissively to problems we don't understand. Science, on the other hand, teaches us to step back, slow down, and ask, simply and dispassionately.

What's going on here?
Why is it happening?
What is causing or influencing it?

Test but Verify

The methodical, logical approach to scientific investigation provides a blueprint for inquiry that rewards reality, not emotion, one step at a time.

Start with the facts. What have you observed or what do you know with a high degree of certainty? Fauci knew from the CDC reports that young gay men were dying of a form of pneumonia that only strikes people whose immune systems have been compromised.

Formulate your question. What's going on and why? Why were these young men dying of a disease that wasn't supposed to attack healthy people? Fauci's team wanted to know.

Develop a hypothesis—your explanation for what you've observed—and test it. In many ways, this hypothesis is the crux of scientific inquiry. The ancient Greek origins of the word offer an explanation. *Hypo* means "foundation," and *thesis* means "placing." Many people confuse hypotheses with theories, thinking they're one and the same. But a hypothesis comes before a theory or explanation. It's the soil below the basement of scientific thought. Charles Darwin had a hypothesis, that plant and animal species originated through competition and "natural selection." Only half a century later, after vast amounts of research and observation, did scientists elevate that hypothesis into a theory: the foundation of an entire field of science. Fauci's hypothesis was that an autoimmune disease was killing these young men, and it was a new disease the world had not previously seen.

Through experimentation, testing, measurement, and documentation Fauci worked to see if his hypothesis held up. Only by submitting ideas to rigorous experimentation, measurement, and scrutiny could he know if the hypothetical ground was stable enough to support the foundation of theory. This meant sharing findings with peers who in turn set out to disprove the hypothesis. Think how different this line of inquiry is from politics and business and so much else in life. So many questions tend to be rhetorical, seeking answers that prove people right—or, at least, on the "right" side. In science, you are trying to prove yourself wrong. The triumph comes when you cannot. It means you have a reasonably stable hypothesis.

If your hypothesis survives this scientific trial by fire, you have an explanation. But even then you haven't achieved total certainty. In science, no answer is ever complete because after your "Why?" is answered, it breeds an infinite number of "Whys." There is more research to be done, new discoveries to make.

These principles—facts, hypothesis, test—can be your guideposts to bring science into your questioning. They will apply in different ways as you connect your observations and facts to your experiments, trying to determine whether your answers hold up to scrutiny. Be prepared to think differently because you have to go into the process embracing uncertainty, reaching into the unknown, knowing answers will take time.

Stretch Yourself

Let's say you had a bad car accident. You came out of it with three broken ribs, whiplash, bad bruises, and persistent pain. You know you're lucky to be alive and still able to move at all, but you hurt like hell. You go to physical therapy and that seems to help, but the pain doesn't go away. Your doctor prescribes pain meds, but you hate them. They send you into orbit, and they don't relieve all the pain anyway. Some friends tell you to try yoga. You read up on it and decide to give it a go. You're desperate, so it's worth the effort. It's not exactly fun and it wipes you out, but after a couple of months, you think you're feeling a little less pain.

Is it the yoga that's making the difference or is your body just healing over time?

You think yoga is working. Maybe yoga can move your body and joints and muscles in ways that minimize the pain from your injury. That's your hypothesis.

You decide to try a little experiment and see if your hypothesis holds up. You stop the yoga. Within a few days, you're pretty sure the pain is getting worse. Sometimes it's hard to tell because it's been such a constant part of your life since the accident. Every day you chart your pain—rating it on a scale of one to ten—when you wake up, at lunchtime, before dinner, and when you go to bed. After a few weeks, you see a trend: Your pain is worse in the morning, after you get up. It goes down around lunch, picks up again around dinner, and ticks up a little more before bedtime. It follows this pattern over several weeks.

You wonder if the morning pain is due to stiffness from sleeping or because you're going to bed with more pain and sleeping poorly. You wonder whether the increase in pain in the evening is because you're just tired and feeling it more, or whether you're feeling the effects of a day's worth of activity. You decide to start the yoga again, this time doing it twice a day—in the morning when you wake up and again just before bed.

After another couple of weeks, you see a change. Your pain still peaks in the morning, but it's down from where it was when you weren't doing the yoga. It still ticks up around dinner, but now it goes back down before bedtime. You conclude yoga twice a day is helping. You can't be 100 percent sure that it's just the yoga. But your chart and your experience indicate a connection between more yoga and less pain.

Congratulations. You did your own simple scientific experiment. And you feel better.

Nina Fedoroff, a plant biologist and former president of the American Association for the Advancement of Science, explained scientific inquiry to me by putting it in terms of "mental constructs," the various ways that disciplines have of interpreting reality. In literature, imagination does the work of making sense of the world. In law, judges use precedents to interpret the law. Science, she says, links ideas to repeated observation and repeatable results of experimentation. The scientist, Fedoroff explains, says okay I have this idea, then asks:

How do I test my idea?
How can my idea be wrong?

In the practical world, there are few incentives to incorporate the mindset that accompanies this type of questioning into our lives and our work. It could be awkward to stand up in front of your boss and say, "Okay, I've got this idea for a new product. But maybe I'm wrong." It would be odd to hear someone at the city council meeting declare, "I know how to make trash pickup more efficient. But we need to test it because I want to see if I'm wrong." Imagine hearing a political candidate say, "I have a plan to raise taxes that will reduce the deficit and save Social Security. But there is some real uncertainty here."

In most cases, we are rewarded for decisiveness and quick answers. The person at the meeting who speaks up with authority and offers to "fix the problem" is often the one who is praised and promoted. When we propose an idea, we don't say to the boss or the shareholders, "I think I'm on to something here, but I'm doing my best to prove it wrong." We're expected to defend our point, not openly invite others to attack it.

The discipline of scientific questioning, however, moves us toward a more methodical form of inquiry, inviting more data and better measurement into the questions we ask and the answers we get. In Silicon Valley, where most everything is measured, one of the most important tools for improving online products is a simple form of experiment called A/B testing. Tech companies try out new features by offering a small percentage of users an updated app while most others use the old one. If the new version performs better—determined by metrics such as how many clicks it gets or how many purchases are made—it's crowned the winner and becomes the version that everyone sees. If not, the better-performing original stays in place. This data-driven approach favors empirical results to pick winning ideas instead of the slickest sales pitch or the most confident employee.

As data becomes more accessible, we can expect more science and more metrics in the decision and questioning process. You have a new product you'd like to put into production. You think you should expand your business overseas to take advantage of a rising global middle class. You're thinking of buying a salmon hatchery in Alaska. Applying some scientific inquiry would force you to slow down in order to observe, hypothesize, experiment, and quantify before leaping to conclusions. Maybe that bed and breakfast in Vermont is the better investment after all.

Slow Answers to Slow Questions

For Tony Fauci, HIV/AIDS research was heartbreakingly frustrating because time was on no one's side. People died while he and other scientists painstakingly went about their work conducting experiments and proving themselves wrong. While researchers were testing and observing, AIDS activists were criticizing and protesting, bearing grim signs reading SILENCE = DEATH. Too little funding, they complained, and too little urgency. Fear and grief and frustration hit hard.

Finally, President George H. W. Bush, who spoke about a "kinder, gentler" America, boosted funding. Fauci put research in high gear. Still, it took three years of intense research before Robert Gallo of NIH and Luc Montagnier from the Pasteur Institute announced that they had identified the virus that causes AIDS—a retrovirus that could incubate in the body for years before erupting into full-blown AIDS.

Once the virus was isolated, researchers went to work to defeat it. Molecular virologists started sequencing it. They examined the genetic code. Then researchers discovered the antibody test, which allowed for prompt diagnosis. They started experimenting with off-the-shelf compounds to see which might inhibit the virus. But it was by no means a straight line. There were false hopes, setbacks, and flat-out failures.

A promising drug, AZT, emerged from this work, and the medical community felt a sudden, uncharacteristic burst of hope that the disease might be reined in. But clinical trials and experience established that AZT lost effectiveness over time because the virus developed resistance to it. Researchers discovered the virus could replicate and mutate, getting around AZT. A setback, which led to a question.

How do we stop the mutation and replication?

Researchers tested more drugs and found that a cocktail of medications, if taken together, could backstop one another and prevent the virus from mutating. The new regime, approved in 1996, increased a patient's expected remaining life from eight months to as much as fifty years. HIV/AIDS still kills, especially in poorer parts of the world. But decades of methodical research—slow questions—paid off. The disease is no longer an automatic death sentence.

Science bases itself on the measurable world. But we can incorporate its method into the way we ask and answer other types of questions to become more precise, more focused, and more accurate. We can slow down, pose our questions more deliberately, and bring more data and facts to the discussion. We can challenge our hypothesis and invite others to do the same in a conscious search for problems with our findings and assumptions.

Scientific questioning can be applied in business, in daily life, and in our communities. Imagine how much more interesting a staff meeting, corporate board retreat, or a policy debate might be if people brought up an idea they had tried to prove wrong before they concluded it was right.

You're thinking about putting money into your company because the competition is out-hustling you. What do your customers want? Where is the demand? What are they buying? As you answer these questions you develop a strategy—a hypothesis—that you can test.

You're not sleeping well. You wake up at two in the morning or can't get to sleep at all. Is it the caffeine, the food, or stress? Before you go to the doctor to do one of those involved sleep studies, what can you figure out on your own? How can you experiment to narrow down the cause of your own insomnia? Perhaps creating a spreadsheet or gathering your data on your own digital fitness tracker, which will tell you when you sleep and how you sleep, will help. Chart your caffeine and exercise, your diet, and your stress level to look for patterns. Come up with a hypothesis and test it.

From outer space to the subatomic particle, scientific questioning probes the real world, trying to figure out real mysteries. It relies on observation and measurement, and it demands patience. It is a humbling form of questioning because it is endless, dwarfed by the universe it seeks to decode.

After studying this line of inquiry, I find myself questioning differently. I think more deeply about what I can see for myself—the observable. I ask more about data, separating what I know from what I think I know. I want to hear more about uncertainty and how we explain and accommodate it. I ask:

What do we see and what do we actually know?
How do we know what we know and how might we explain it?
Could we be wrong, and what's the next question to ask?

CHAPTER 10

THE EDISON TEST

Interview Questions

THE QUESTIONS MOST OF US know best but fear most are the questions that take place in the job interview. Whether you're on the receiving end—trying to get the job—or on the giving end—trying to fill the job—the questions that get asked and answered here have real and immediate consequence. As a candidate, if you botch the answer to an important question, you don't get hired. If you're the boss and you fail to ask the right questions, you can miss a critical piece of information and hire the wrong person.

Successful job interviews revolve around a coherent set of questions that assess talent and accomplishment, examine judgment and values, consider success and failure, sample personality, and explore compatibility. Some of the questions are straightforward. Those are the fastballs. They come right across the plate and ask directly about previous experience or skills. Others are more unpredictable. They are the curveballs. They can come out of nowhere and test your reflexes and imagination. They may ask about something seemingly unrelated or frivolous. Either way, when you hit one out of the park, everyone cheers.

The first rule of the job interview: Don't wing it. Preparation pays. Know what you're talking about and to whom. Know as much as possible about the job. Have a list of questions on a pad and in your head. Think about where you're going in the conversation, what you want to find out, and how you want to get there. Just as you wouldn't sail across the Atlantic without GPS, you don't approach a job interview without strategy and structure. You are not sitting down for a random chat. You are trying to learn as much about the other person as you can to establish whether this position is fit for both of you.

If you're the applicant, you can anticipate that most every interview will ask you touchstone questions about your background, your professional experience, your interests, and what you bring to the table.

> *Why are you interested in this position?*
> *What do you think you can do for us?*
> *What makes you qualified and unique?*
> *Why should we hire you?*

Prepare a series of responses for each question. Organize your thoughts in bullet points, two or three distinct characteristics for each response, so you can talk about several traits without getting lost or long-winded. Practice your answers. You want to be clear and concise, prepared to address the question—or a variation of it—directly and confidently. Think of some examples or short stories that highlight relevant experience or set you apart. If you led a group of people to China to study architectural design and energy efficiency, you can talk about the new materials and technologies you saw and the discussion you had about China's changing culture of innovation. If you ran a summer camp and had to deal with screaming kids and demanding parents, you can talk about the lessons of human nature that you so ably put to use to keep everyone happy.

Keep in mind that to the astute interviewer, your tone will convey as much about you as the words you use, so strike a balance in how you present yourself. Talk about your successes without bragging, express confidence without sounding cocky, acknowledge your shortcomings without sounding insecure. Be prepared to speak about your character and personality by citing a tough decision or a dilemma you faced and how you worked your way through it. Know what questions you want to ask. The questions that you, the candidate, will ask are nearly as important as your answers to the interviewer's questions. You need to project informed curiosity about the position, the enterprise, the competitive landscape, and the measures of success.

You've been hiring a lot of people lately. What's driving your growth?

How has your digital strategy affected your retail strategy?

How do your employees translate the corporate social responsibility you promote into their own work lives?

How are you doing with your questions and your answers? The best way to know is to listen to yourself. So try practicing by recording your answers on your smartphone. Do one answer at a time. Take it from someone who has done TV all his life—watching and listening to yourself is a sobering experience! You'll be your harshest critic, but the experience will allow you to modulate your voice and fine-tune your answers so you project confidence and fluency.

If you're the interviewer, you hope your candidates have practiced their responses. You want them to impress you, to talk about their strengths and why they're the perfect fit for the job you're filling. So you have to ask precisely and persistently to get beyond the résumé and practiced responses. Tailor the questions to the candidate and the job. If you're filling a management position, ask about how your applicant deals with people, motivates success, and handles setbacks. If the job requires physical endurance, ask about similar work the candidate has done and how he stayed healthy. You are asking questions that call for tangible answers that shed light on your applicant's talent, experience, and personality. You want to get a sense of what will motivate her and keep her productive. You ask about situations or experiences that illuminate intangible characteristics, such as how the person deals with adversity or thinks creatively. You want insight into the other person's work ethic and professional expectations, goals, and ambitions.

What's the most successful project you've run?
What is it about this job that interests you most?
How does this job connect with your larger professional aspirations?

Both the interviewer and the interviewee have an interest in clarifying the expectations of the workplace and establishing the qualities that each party brings to the relationship. Both try to dig out information by using direct lines of inquiry and by listening to words and tone. Both are asking themselves:

Will this be a good fit?
Do our skills and interests align?
Do we want the same things?
Are we compatible?

Job interview questions that look for compatibility come in some basic shapes and sizes. They ask you to:

Introduce yourself. These questions ask who you are, what you've accomplished, what you've learned. They ask about background and qualifications, where you've been, and where you're going. They reveal what makes you unique.

Share your vision. Imagine that you are already on the job and part of the team. Take a situation, an opportunity, or a crisis and say how you would meet it. What risks would you take? Apply your past experience and knowledge to the new and imagined challenge.

Acknowledge setbacks and challenges. These questions go to the hard things in life—the really tough decisions, the failures, and the conflicts. This line of inquiry explores the human story and the adversity that calls for ingenuity, fortitude, and resilience.

Swing at the curveball. Think fast! These out-of-the blue questions test spontaneity and creative thought. They push people out of their prepared responses to get to the unvarnished and the genuine. Be creative. Be genuine. Have some fun.

Hunting the Best Heads

To get an inside perspective on the questions that job interviewers value most, I called Shelly Storbeck, managing partner of Storbeck/ Pimentel and Associates, an executive search firm that specializes in higher education and nonprofit recruitment. I'd met Shelly years before when I was a candidate in a search. She is a keen judge of character and a realist about what it takes to be a leader in academia, where every stakeholder needs to be heard. Change is difficult when tenured faculty, defiant students, helicopter parents, and tradition-loving alumni have a say. There can be as many constituencies on campus as there are in a good-sized city.

Shelly leads her candidates through multiple rounds of interviewing, questioning, and probing in the first screening before recommending them to the next phases of the hunt. Then search committees, senior administrators, faculty, students, and staff submit applicants to days of questioning to determine if they have the vision and fit the institution intellectually, professionally, and emotionally.

In her interviewing, Shelly cuts right to the chase. If it's a presidential search, she asks the candidate to talk about his or her experience pursuing presidential goals—fundraising, governance, enrollment, raising academic quality. She asks for specifics. If increasing diversity is a priority, for example, she asks:

How have you pursued diversity?
Who and how many diverse candidates have you actually hired?
How did you get robust candidate pools?
How did you mentor the people you brought on board?

To tap into a candidate's vision, Shelly asks what she calls "magic wand" questions to draw out the big ideas that leadership confers—potentially game-changing ideas that can bend an institution's trajectory and change its culture.

> *If you had a magic wand here, what would you do with it?*
> *How would you work with different constituencies?*
> *What is your ambition for this institution and how would you achieve it?*

The magic wand invites the user to skip over politics and bureaucracy and think creatively.

If red flags have come up through reference checks, Shelly asks about those, too. She asks artfully, seeking candor and reflection rather than defensiveness or evasion. Knowing that everyone on a university or college campus has an opinion and just about every leader gets criticized by someone, she might ask:

> *What would your detractors say about you?*

A self-aggrandizing answer masquerading as self-criticism doesn't cut it. *"I work too hard and people don't like it when I send out emails at 3 a.m."* is not what she's looking for. She wants honesty and realism; she listens for a thoughtful response that suggests the candidate is aware of her foibles and cares about how they play with the people around her. She considers this essential because the complexity of an executive's job requires a tapestry of relationships to build consensus.

"Self-awareness is essential to being a successful leader," Shelly explained to me.

Look Back, Look Ahead

Job interview questions fall into two constructs: what you have done and what you will do. The first kind, *behavioral questions*, ask a candidate to look back on what he or she has accomplished, achieved, or attempted.

These questions dig into the lessons that time and experience have imparted.

> *Can you provide an example of when you set a goal and a timetable and achieved them?*
>
> *Give me an example of how you responded when your boss asked you for advice or asked you to do something that you disagreed with.*
>
> *What's the hardest decision you've had to make at work, and how did you go about it?*

These questions help shed light on how a job candidate has behaved under specific circumstances. They probe for details. But more than merely revisiting the past, they explore dilemmas and decisions that reveal ethics and values. The ways a candidate confronted a difficult challenge or dealt with a setback indicate how she might deal with problems in the new job.

Because past performance does not necessarily predict future results, good interviews also include *situational questions*. These future-oriented questions seek to reveal how a candidate would look forward and respond to a potential decision or situation. The best questions combine the particulars of a situation with a challenging choice.

> *Suppose your company had a very good year. You've been asked how the additional profits should be spent. What would you recommend?*
>
> *If you were told that all departments had to cut 5 percent in spending and you were responsible for the budget, how would you decide where to cut?*
>
> *A coworker tells you that she thinks she is not being paid fairly, that other people at about the same level of work are making more than she is. Now what?*
>
> *There is a project the boss believes in passionately but that you think is ill-advised and may even get the company in trouble. You have a meeting to discuss it. What do you say?*

These questions help establish quality of character and how candidates can imagine their way through adversity. They ask the candidate to connect aspirations and thought process to illuminate how he or she would draw on experience, logic, integrity, and understanding of the issues to make a decision.

Finding Innovation

Interviews for management and creative jobs ask how you will imagine, lead, or innovate. It seems that every company trumpets innovation these days, so how does an interviewer bring out innovation in an applicant? How does the successful applicant answer such questions?

I thought Jean Case would be a good person to consult. She and her husband, Steve Case, helped ignite the technology revolution back in the 1990s when Steve cofounded America Online. Back then, we ponderously referred to the internet as the World Wide Web. AOL brought it into just about everyone's home. The company became synonymous with the emerging new world of digital communication and connection. Jean was a senior executive and helped make AOL one of the world's most recognized and transformational companies.

In the late 1990s, as AOL approached its zenith, Steve and Jean Case created the Case Foundation. I first met them when AOL bought Time Warner, which owned CNN. The merger proved to be a disaster, but the Case Foundation, run by Jean, lives on, bringing people and technology together with philanthropy and business to push for social change. The Case Foundation sees itself as a convener of innovators. I wanted to know how the Cases found the people to do the work and inspire the change they sought. What did they ask in order to assemble a creative, original, technologically dexterous team?

I met Jean for lunch at a cramped but trendy seafood place in Washington. She arrived practically at a run, with a big, broad smile and a whoosh of energy, one hand clutching her smartphone, the other outstretched in greeting. She dove into conversation.

I expected her to be data- and metrics-driven, with a predetermined list of questions that probed the applicants' experience, asked about what they had invented, and tested their technological competence. I was wrong. Jean wants to learn as much about *how* people think as *what* they think and know.

Jean is impatient. You see that instantly. She speaks fast and about big ideas. She is active in many causes—from planetary health to brain health. She's served on school boards and presidential commissions. She doesn't have time to waste. So when she asks questions of a job candidate, she expects precision and speed. She wants to know if the candidate has done his homework and has something original to say. She asks:

What have we gotten right?
What haven't we gotten right?
What's missing?
If you were sitting in my chair, what would you have done?

She asks about decisions the candidate has made or actions he has taken that are out of the ordinary. She is listening for answers that indicate the candidate can think fast and pivot when an opportunity or a setback changes the equation. She's looking for risk takers.

How comfortable are you with unplanned surprises that come
* along?*
Are you bold enough to put on the table an idea that's fearless
* when you don't have the data to know it will work?*
Can you make a compelling case as to why you should
* try it?*

These are Jean's fastball questions. They test the candidate's thought process and ask for logic and imagination about an unfamiliar situation or scenario. Jean's fastballs reflect real-world concerns and dilemmas— a business decision, a personnel issue, an investment opportunity, a technology play—that relate directly to the candidate's experiences and aspirations.

If you get the opportunity, how will you solve the problem?
How will you be smarter and stronger if it works?
How will you learn from it if it doesn't work?

Like Shelly Storbeck, Jean asks about a candidate's setbacks and short-comings. She wants to hear how he discusses adversity or a particular challenge that didn't turn out perfectly. She wants to hear how he dealt with disappointment or rallied when the team did not perform well. She asks the question bluntly:

What's been your worst failure?

"It's amazing how many people want to hide from that question," Jean tells me, explaining that she views failure, dealt with wisely and described sincerely, as an asset. In the right context, failure represents a willingness to try something new and untested. Every applicant, Jean believes, should come prepared to talk about a failure.

What did you learn from it?

Fastball questions can be highly effective in job interviews, but they also work in other contexts. As an interviewer, I ask this type of question a lot—whether I'm speaking with a mayor, a mother, a CEO, or a teacher—because I want to know how people think and handle crises. As Shelly Storbeck observed, the right questions prompt candidates to provide lessons from their own narrative.

Be Ready for the Curveball

Pitchers can't live by fastballs alone, and the same applies in interviews and job talks. When I interview candidates (for jobs or for politics) I like to throw curveballs too, to shake things up and test the candidate's spon-taneity. Curveball questions can come out of the blue—an unexpected topic or sudden shift. Serious or funny, curveballs should be different from your run-of-the-mill interview questions. They are looking for an unrehearsed response, a little humor, or some humanizing insight into the candidate's personality and thought process.

In newsmaker interviews, I throw curveballs for similar effect. I remember an interview I was doing at The George Washington University with Michael Hayden, the former CIA director and retired four-star Air Force general. We were talking about desperately serious things—terrorism, cyberattacks, and rising threats from China and Russia. It was fascinating and it was important. But I also wanted the audience to get to know Hayden as a human being, to have a sense of how he thought, decided, and relaxed. I knew Hayden had a dry sense of humor, so partway through the discussion I paused, turned to the audience, and noted that even CIA directors get time off. He was the nation's top spook. I asked:

Spy movies . . . TV shows. What do you watch?

Hayden lit up. *"Homeland,"* he replied with a smile. The show revolves around a bipolar CIA operative, Carrie Mathison, alternately brilliant and unhinged. Hayden knew people in the CIA just like that, he said. He worked right alongside them. He went on to talk about life inside the CIA and how he managed the pressures of that intense 24/7 job with the normal life that no one much thought about. For just a few minutes, the conversation came back down to earth. Hayden was funny and approachable. My question wasn't brilliant, just a little different, an intentional pause in the intense discussion we'd been having, an effort to let the conversation—and the guest—breathe.

Curveball questions are often a part of job interviews. Jean Case told me she throws curveballs to see how people react and whether they can answer spontaneously and creatively. "We want to see how they respond when we ask them very nonobvious and unexpected kinds of things," she said. Since originality and creativity are attributes she seeks in her applicants, she pays special attention to the answers. One of her favorite questions is:

What's your favorite aisle at the grocery store?

I thought about her supermarket question and how I'd answer it personally. Maybe I'd go for the coffee aisle. The shelves show how deliciously diverse the world is, from Ethiopian Yergacheffe to Two Volcanoes Guatemalan. It's an aromatic reminder that each day should start with a flavorful celebration. There's evidence of human inventiveness and innovation—drip and espresso and single cup—amid the complexity of globalization and the challenges of human labor. The rise of organic and fair market coffees suggests that change is possible and prosperity can be shared. Coffee, you might say, is a metaphor for our times.

Don't know if it would get me Case's job, but maybe I'd qualify to be a barista somewhere.

The Candid Candidate

Job interviews often happen in intimidating or artificial surroundings— in front of a search committee or in a paneled office. The best candidates come confident and well prepared. Having practiced their answers and anticipated the questions, they walk in with their brains crammed with carefully crafted responses. It's understandable. But the most fruitful interview ends with a genuine sense of the real candidate, not the one projected in the perfectly planned out answers.

No one is better rehearsed than political candidates running for office. Interviews with political candidates are simply public job interviews.

Why do you want this job?
What have you done to deserve it?
What will you do if you get it?

The most public job interview of all, the U.S. presidential debate, puts the candidates side by side, with a bunch of cameras recording every moment. While no reasonable employer would ask applicants to submit themselves to a routine like this, these debates offer some interesting lessons to consider. The most important one: Candidates want to stay on message. They ignore questions they don't like. They say what they think people want to hear. So the interviewer should know it may take two or three swipes at a topic to pry loose an answer to the question at hand.

I decided to visit Bob Schieffer, someone who spent years trying to cut through canned responses for a living. He worked for CBS News for nearly half a century and hosted the network's Sunday interview program, *Face the Nation*, for fourteen years. He moderated three presidential debates—Bush-Kerry in 2004, Obama-McCain in 2008, and Obama-Romney in 2012.

Imperturbable, with a good-old-boy southern smooth about him, Schieffer was one of the most dedicated, straight-shooting journalists of his time. His goal in the debate-as-job-interview was to get candidates to offer some insight on how they'd handle the job, the decisions they'd make, and the character they'd bring to it. Schieffer had years of practice interviewing people who were frustratingly disciplined at staying on message, sometimes ignoring questions entirely in order to say what they wanted to say. His challenge was to get his guests to do more than rehash their focus group–tested talking points.

Schieffer's advice to candidates and questioners alike: be direct and be yourself. Be genuine. A highly effective interviewer, Schieffer was always known for his straightforward, conversational style. He never projected the self-important, smart guy approach that typified many pundits and talk-show hosts. In his debate questions, Schieffer tried for a more three-dimensional view of the candidates by mixing topics and alternating questions about policy.

He recalled one exchange in 2004, when George W. Bush was running for reelection against challenger John Kerry. The country was at war in Afghanistan and Iraq. Schieffer asked Bush a question of faith.

"Mr. President . . . you were asked . . . after the invasion of Iraq if you had checked with your dad. And I believe you said you had checked with a higher authority," Schieffer said. "What part does your faith play on your policy decisions?"

Schieffer knew Bush often invoked his religious faith and that faith was an important part of life for millions of Americans. It was also part of Bush's personal narrative of redemption. Schieffer also knew the stories suggesting that Bush went to war in Iraq to settle an old score for his father, who cast a daunting shadow over the Bush boys. Schieffer touched three live wires—faith, family, and war—and stepped back to see what would happen.

Bush didn't give away the store, but his answer provided some texture and insight into how he thought and how his faith sustained him. Yes, he said, faith played a "big part" in his life, and he prayed a lot:

"I pray for wisdom. I pray for our troops in harm's way. I pray for my family. I pray for my little girls. But I'm mindful in a free society that people can worship if they want to or not. You're equally an American if you choose to worship an Almighty and if you choose not to. If you're a Christian, Jew, or Muslim you're equally an American. The great thing about America is the right to worship the way you see fit."

He didn't duck the question.

"Prayer and religion sustain me," Bush said. "I receive calmness in the storms of the presidency . . . I never want to impose my religion on anybody else. But when I make decisions I stand on principle. And the principles are derived from who I am."

Schieffer could have pressed harder. He could have followed up. But whatever a viewer thought of Bush or religion and prayer, Schieffer's question offered Bush an opportunity to talk about an important aspect of his life. I don't recommend asking a question about faith in a job interview unless you want your friends in HR all over you. But in presidential politics all is fair game, and Schieffer's question brought together the personal, the professional, and the provocative to ask about philosophy and motivation.

History will determine George W. Bush's stature among presidents. The public will decide whether it hired the right man at the right time. But in that moment, in front of a search committee of more than 50 million viewers, whether they liked the response or not, the public got a sense of Bush's attitude toward faith and how he explained its role in his decision making. It wasn't ground-breaking but it provided texture, and in the context of the presidential job interview, texture adds interest and insight.

If you want to know what drives your candidate, you can fashion a question that explores similarly complex terrain. Connect a decision to principles and values. Ask in a curious but matter-of-fact way. Know why you're asking, and what you're listening for.

Asking for the Team

Active listening drives good job interviews. It focuses in on compatibility markers such as complementary experience, shared interests, interpersonal skills, integrity, work ethic and a sense of professional mission. Experienced job interviewers listen for experience that corresponds to the job. They listen for insight into personality traits—energy, creativity, imagination, humor, risk tolerance—that align with the culture of the place.

For Jim Davis, CEO of New Balance, much revolves around teamwork. Jim has been an athlete all his life and is a naturally competitive guy. When he bought New Balance in 1972, it employed six people and was making thirty pairs of shoes a day. When we spoke, New Balance employed more than 6,000 people worldwide and was a $4 billion enterprise doing business in 140 countries. It still made its shoes in America.

Jim told me that he was always more of a listener than a talker. He shunned the spotlight. But he knew what he wanted and where he was going. Focused and confident, he explained that he built his business over the years by assembling a team he trusts. He believes that "the team" is a company's most important asset, and he approaches his recruiting like the general manager of a major league franchise. He looks for exceptional talent but thinks about where and how he needs it and the effect it will have on the overall effort. He asks candidates directly how they function in a team environment.

How have you applied that approach?
How have you worked within a group to solve problems?

If a candidate shows too much ego or doesn't sound like a team player, Jim told me, "We pass." He listens intently for pronouns. He wants to hear "we," not "I." It is an indicator, he's discovered over the years, of an approach as well as an attitude. "You can't do things yourself," he explained to me. "You can't do anything sustainable yourself."

Jim raised an important point in his pronoun patrol. The distinction between "I" and "we" is real. Individual initiative and accomplishment are important. They represent a track record and help answer the what-will-you-do-for-us question. But "we" sends a powerful signal, too, showing awareness of the team and a willingness to share the glory. It conveys inclusiveness, concern, and respect for the group and a generosity of spirit that can inspire others. Who wouldn't want a person like that on the team?

Interview the Interviewer

When I interview job applicants, I learn a lot about them from the questions they ask of me. Some of the most important questions in a job interview come from that other side of the table. Curiosity and compatibility are mutual. These questions reveal whether a candidate has done his homework, how deep down he has drilled, and what his priorities and interests are. If a candidate starts with questions about pay, benefits, or vacation, he conveys a lack of interest in the job itself. Shelly Storbeck, the executive headhunter, told me that the most effective candidate questions reflect a sophisticated curiosity and passion for the job.

What are your traditions and what is sacred?
What will be the hardest things to change?

Cindy Holland, head of content acquisition at Netflix, helped revolutionize the way the world consumes media. She's responsible for shows that millions of people around the world binge-watch—shows like *Orange Is the New Black*, *House of Cards*, and *Narcos*. Holland was profiled in the *New York Times* Corner Office column for her accomplishments and management style. Always looking for independent, creative thinkers—the kind of people who will help Netflix find the next big hit—Holland sometimes starts by turning the tables in the opening scene, starting with:

What questions do you have for me?

Holland told the *Times* she wants to know that job candidates have done their homework, have passion, and are curious. "I want to know what they're interested in and where they come from and what they're seeking to do." She listens closely and judges quickly: "Some people respond well to that first question and some people are so thrown that they say they don't have any questions. It doesn't disqualify them automatically, but it definitely tells me something about them."

Jean Case believes that candidates demonstrate confidence and courage in the questions they ask. She told me about one candidate who pushed so hard and asked so many insistent questions about the Case Foundation that it made her uncomfortable. "She was challenging me," said Case. "There was one part of me that hated it and another part of me that said, 'Oh, she is so right for this organization.'"

Do you know when you have impact?
How are you sure?
What's the discipline you use to know the value of what
you've done?

The candidate insistently asked about one of the toughest issues a foundation faces. Those questions led to a long conversation about metrics, accountability, and impact. The candidate got the job.

Jean counsels business students to "be fearless" in their job interviews and ask if they'll have creative running room.

What freedom do I have to step outside the defined role?
How much do you want to hear from me when I am not asked?
What impact do you want to have in the world?
Where does that stand as a priority in your business plan?

I once sent a student to speak to an accomplished friend who was running an exciting startup and looking for promising young talent. The student had done well in class and I thought the two of them might hit it off. About a week after they met, I reached out to my friend to see how things went.

"To be completely honest, it was bad," he said. "The student was nice, but she had no idea who she was talking to or what we were trying to do here." She seemed unaware of my friend's contributions to the field. She never asked how he was applying his experiences or where he wanted to take the business. She did not get the job.

Good job candidates ask serious questions that reflect deep prepa- ration, a grasp of the organization, and a genuine desire for the job. Candidates should study up on the business and its competitive environ- ment. Know about the top people as well as your prospective boss and the interviewer. Ask about the specifics of the job, organizational goals, past experience, and current prospects. Demonstrate informed curiosity about the challenges, opportunities, and culture of the place. What you ask, and how you ask it, projects your knowledge, interest, and engage- ment. Write down ten smart questions and be prepared to ask them. Make some of the questions open-ended and some very specific. Role- play the likely answers and have some follow-on questions.

You took a hit from the competition last year. How are you dealing with that?
I know there's been a big shift to online. How has that changed the culture of the place?
Where do you see the biggest challenges and opportunities in the next five years?

Bright Ideas

Job interviews have evolved. In the 1920s, Thomas Edison found himself inundated with job applicants. Being the inventive guy he was, Edison created a test with 141 questions to help him choose the best candidates. They went from the simple to the scientific:

> *What countries bound France?*
> *How fast does sound travel per foot per second?*
> *Name three principal acids.*

Ninety percent of the job applicants failed. The questionnaire prompted an uproar. "Edison Questions Stir Up a Storm," read a headline in the *New York Times* on May 11, 1921. "Victims of Test Say Only a Walking Encyclopedia Could Answer Questionnaire." Still, there's little doubt that the test winnowed down the number of candidates.

The job interview has progressed since Edison's day. Now companies use sophisticated "predictive analytics" to measure responses against likely outcomes to forecast retention, learning capacity, leadership potential, and the ability to innovate and make effective decisions. Some companies require candidates to record Skype statements. But determining compatibility—finding Jim Davis's team chemistry—still depends on human interaction, and that's driven by the questions that get asked.

Want some practice? You might try the questions at the online dating site eHarmony. Seriously. These questions represent a sort of job interview for romance. More than 100 questions seek insight and reflection on basic traits and hidden quirks.

> *What adjectives describe you?*
> *How do you rate your emotions?*
> *Do you feel better when you're around other people?*

I'm not recommending hiring by way of online dating. But these compatibility questions, which ask who you are, where you're headed, and how you describe yourself, are designed to prompt the lovelorn to articulate what they're all about. They're great practice for a job interview!

Here's one everyone should answer:

Do you ask questions when you are in search of information?

CHAPTER 11

THE INSPIRED HOST

Entertaining Questions

BEING A TALK-SHOW HOST IS FUN. You meet interesting people. You get to ask them about their work and their lives, probe their past, and ask them to tell stories. You push them and get personal, test their mettle, and find the funny. You can go for the reflective and thoughtful, or you can be tough and demanding, asking why your guest did what she did when she did it. It's your call because it's your show. You set the agenda. You own the space.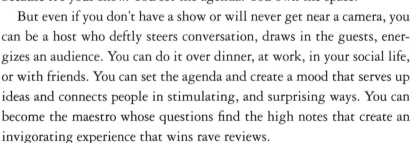

But even if you don't have a show or will never get near a camera, you can be a host who deftly steers conversation, draws in the guests, energizes an audience. You can do it over dinner, at work, in your social life, or with friends. You can set the agenda and create a mood that serves up ideas and connects people in stimulating, and surprising ways. You can become the maestro whose questions find the high notes that create an invigorating experience that wins rave reviews.

Entertaining questions allow you to engage your audience and keep the conversation interesting and lively so everyone plays. You can be commanding or charming, funny or unpredictable, but the objective always revolves around creating an experience that your guests will enjoy and remember. Use questions the same way a chef uses spices: subtly but deliberately to bring out the flavors of the meal. Basic ingredients?

Know your audience. Who you are talking to? What have they done? Where have they been and what do they care about? Pick questions that intrigue and interest everyone.

Think creatively, choose deliberately. Draw from a menu of topics and questions to create flow and distinctive moments. Sports or politics, fishing or sailing, it's up to you, but you want a combination of topics that will engage different people on different levels. It's like the meal: plates filled with flavors and colors, veggies and proteins.

Set a mood and set a rhythm. Funny or serious? Provocative or reflective? Set the mood through signals, prompts, words, and timing.

Engage emotion. You trigger emotions through the subjects you pick and the questions you ask. Serious or snide? Funny or flippant? Your call.

I find that if I start with an exchange that is spontaneous and a little unexpected, I can often break the ice, get a smile, and set a tone that is more relaxed and will lead to a more genuine experience.

I was hosting one of my *Conversation Series* events at The George Washington University, onstage with House Minority Leader and former House Speaker Nancy Pelosi. I had interviewed Pelosi before and knew her reasonably well. I had a bunch of things I wanted to ask her about—politics, the economy, climate change, Washington's weird ways. In doing my research, I had been warned, very diplomatically, that Pelosi was prone to long, sometimes slightly meandering answers. I didn't want that. I was looking for a genuine conversation that would cover a lot of ground and illuminate both her politics and her personality. I wanted to draw her out on the polarization in the country and what she could do to change that. I wanted her to talk about how (and why) anyone would go into politics. Mostly, though, I wanted her to engage in a spontaneous and conversational way with me and with the audience.

I decided to start by asking if she'd be willing to begin with a little game.

She looked at me quizzically. "Whatever you wish," she said warily.

Okay, I said, "I'll give you a name or a topic, you get a one-word response."

"Do I get the same?" she asked with a grin.

"Absolutely!" I responded. The audience laughed in anticipation.

Pelosi leaned forward, watching intently, not knowing exactly where this was going. I wasn't going to pounce or embarrass her, but I was trying to put some energy in the exchange and drive some spontaneity to the conversation.

Just the night before, Pelosi had been on the front lines of a big budget deal. It was Republican House Speaker John Boehner's swan song achievement, his last big act before retiring. It passed with votes from Republicans and Democrats alike—a rare event in Washington. Pelosi had rallied support from her side. That's where I started.

"Budget deal?" I asked.

"Hooray," was her reply. She smiled proudly.

The presidential campaign was under way and an unlikely candidate was leading the Republican field. I invoked his name.

"Donald Trump?" I asked.

"Performer." She grimaced.

Abroad, Vladimir Putin was rattling sabers, deploying his military.

"Russia?"

"Careful." She scowled.

Democrats are perennially on the defensive about big government. Their adversaries like to refer to them as tax-and-spend liberals.

"Taxes?"

Pelosi paused. "Investment."

Democrats wanted to raise taxes to pay for a range of government programs, so that one word captured their rationale perfectly. In less than a minute, we'd covered several topics—and with an amusing economy of Qs and As. Our political word association game opened the conversation with a few laughs and no speeches, and it established an informal and approachable relationship onstage. It encouraged spontaneity and set Pelosi's internal clock and her expectations for how I was going to proceed. I think she enjoyed it. I know the audience did because I heard their reaction and laughter and I knew my questions touched on a variety of issues they were following in the news.

Opening with scene-setter questions can help you get people talking, set the pace, and frame the conversation. Figure out what you want to talk about and how, factor in the personalities you have in the room, then map out questions and anticipated responses. You can excite the imagination or you can prompt reflection. It's your show.

Would you buy a Tesla?
Who's the most inspiring person you've ever met and why?

Set the Stage, Set the Tone

When it comes to hosting, I've never met anybody quite like Chris Schroeder. An entrepreneur and an investor, Chris was a digital pioneer, leading WashingtonPost.com in its early days. He invested in a health-related website, built it big, then sold it for a handsome profit. He traveled the world to meet young entrepreneurs who are redefining technology and globalization, and wrote a book.

Chris is a question *machine*. He recalled that as a young boy, he spent hours with his Italian grandmother, watching her cook, smelling the aromatic tapestry of pastas and meat, onions and garlic, spices and herbs, and asking all he could about the recipes and the family. What was in it? How did she make it? Where did it come from? Where were *they* from?

Ever since I've known him, Chris has been like that—asking incessantly, deeply, about people, ideas, events, and the world around us. He's an intense and caring magnet for other people as well. They seek his advice because he listens and he asks persistently about opportunities and obstacles, vulnerabilities, and trade-offs.

Exploding with ideas, Chris is driven by his manic curiosity. In his book *Startup Rising*, he argued that young people in the Middle East embracing technology and innovation will ultimately transform the region in positive and profound ways. For all the turmoil, Chris believes young twenty-first-century innovators are hard at work and will bend history toward knowledge and progress. He is a stubborn optimist.

About twice a month, Chris and his wife, Sandy, host a dinner party. He is a blue-jeans casual, Harvard-educated guy whose interests run from food and sports to technology and foreign policy. Having inherited his grandmother's love of cooking, he serves up fresh pasta, great wine, homemade everything accompanied by a feast of ideas. His dinner parties are a cross between *Top Chef* and *Meet the Press*. On this night, the menu featured fresh pasta amatriciana, lamb stew with mint, and four wines from Italy. He'd sent an email to all the guests twenty-four hours earlier, commenting, "Several of you have asked kindly if you can bring anything, and the answer is no, except an Uber if you will be enjoying some of our wine."

But think about this, he wrote:

> *What is something you see in your world that blows you away right now?*
> *Or, what is obvious in your world that to the rest of us may be extremely unobvious?*
> *By the third wine . . . we may figure out how to save the entire world . . .*

Five couples gathered that Saturday evening at Schroeder's home, big and warm and welcoming. He and Sandy made gracious introductions, since some of the guests had never met. After some socializing, we moved into the dining room for the main event.

Chris served. Sandy was happy to let him run the show. Their teenage son helped, pouring water and wine, lingering when something caught his ear. After welcoming all of us to his table, Chris slid into his role as host, first offering an observation, followed by a gust of questions. Traveling for his book had given him remarkable access and taken him to places few could visit. He'd just returned from Iran, a place that had dominated headlines and American foreign policy since Islamic revolutionaries stormed the American embassy in Tehran and took hostages in 1979. But now what? Chris told us he had met a new generation of young innovators churning with aspiration, anxious to play, defiant in their ideas, and believing in change. These entrepreneurs were more connected and more empowered than ever, using technology to network with like-minded young people. He saw them collaborating online with other entrepreneurs and innovators around the world. If they had a smartphone, they were not restricted by physical frontiers or cultural expectations. Chris told the story of a young woman who was trying to finance her software startup. She was raising the money to bring her idea to market. And there were thousands like her.

He turned to the table. None of us had been to Iran but he threw out some questions we all could chew on.

> *How will kids—connected by satellite TV, the internet, and*
> *smartphones—change the equation?*
> *How disruptive can they be?*
> *How can any government manage the expectations of this young,*
> *globally networked generation?*
> *Could we imagine how things might play out as mullahs are*
> *challenged by millennials? What should America and the*
> *world do in response?*

The table lit up.

The government will build a better firewall, predicted one person.

The kids will find a way around it, said someone else.

Governments cannot keep up with technology or with youth, offered a third.

The ayatollahs still control the country.

The world should lay low and let things play out. Young people have already created a parallel universe where they just ignore what they don't like. Change from within is inevitable.

Too risky. The hard-liners will never let it happen.

Everyone had a place in the conversation, whether they followed what was going on in Iran or not, because Chris's questions touched on the universal themes of youth, technology, communication, and the process of change as much as they invoked the particulars and politics of Iran. His questions invited participation at whatever level the guests felt comfortable. He selected a topic he cared about and then framed it in a way that was approachable and real. Most people don't talk about Iran, but who hadn't thought about the impact of smartphones and social media in the hands of kids and how they are shaping the future?

The courses came and went and the wine flowed with the topics, as Chris changed direction or deferred to a guest who had an observation on an altogether different slice of life. Spontaneity had a place at the table, too.

"They're not teaching handwriting in school anymore," observed one of the young parents, shocked at her own recent discovery. "Cursive will be a lost art."

> *What are we losing if no one learns handwriting?*
> *What about the connection between hand, heart, and the creative*
> *soul?*

Someone had read an article about how handwriting influences reading, writing, and language; soon several of us plunged into a discussion about the virtues of analog relics like pen and paper, hard copy, and real books. Each of us came at the discussion from our own perspective, and each expressed a slightly different view. But everyone seemed to agree in the end that those mindless handwriting exercises actually served a purpose, forcing us to slow down and write between the lines— an enduring gift, perhaps, in an age of digital transience.

It was time for coffee, dessert, and that email question that Chris had sent the night before.

> *What is not obvious that just blows you away?*

We'd all had time to think about it and the answers were all over the map. New technology for the disabled, said one person. Drones, suggested another. But it was Pradeep's answer that drew everyone in: Air-conditioning.

Air-conditioning?

Yes, said Pradeep. He had recently visited his ancestral village in the state of Tamil Nadu in southern India. He was born and lived there until he was six or so, when he moved with his parents to the United States. His village was a small, remote place of maybe 10,000 people. A few streets passed through the village, crossing near the big temple in town. One of those roads then went down to the river. For centuries the economy revolved around rice, bananas, and mangoes. Lush and deep green, the place had always been defined by its oppressive heat, often exceeding 100 paralyzing degrees.

"I remember in my childhood you would not leave the house during huge chunks of the day," Pradeep told me later. "Maybe inside you had a fan, but outside it was 100 and you wouldn't be able to do anything."

He'd visited periodically as he was growing up and through his college years, but, until his recent visit, he hadn't been back in fifteen years. He found the changes amazing—an explosion of roads, cars, construction, and smartphones. And that not-so-obvious thing that he now realized had made such a difference was air-conditioning. Air-conditioning meant the place could be tamed, the environment modified. There were now cool spaces where people could work, study, and linger. Yes, Pradeep told us, the air-conditioning that we so take for granted in much of the world had made his ancient village habitable and transformed a way of life that had remained basically constant for thousands of years. Sure, there was still poverty. But this village was morphing from an isolated, subsistence backwater to a modernizing, connected community.

Pradeep's story enthralled us. He made it personal and real. We learned about him and his ancestral home. He spoke of human progress and connected us to a place no one else had seen. We shared his amazement and discovery. He made us care about his little village and, yes, air-conditioning.

The evening concluded with enthusiastic praise for great food, remarkable conversation, and the new friends we'd made around the table. Chris had been a deft host, dishing up ideas and questions that engaged the room, took us around the world, and got everyone talking. Chris made dinner an event.

You're On!

Good hosts are always on, always listening, and always interested in their guests and the conversation around them. Their curiosity roadmap reveals their interest in people, places, and ideas. Jimmy Fallon, Ellen DeGeneres, Anderson Cooper, and Terry Gross are powerful personalities themselves, but their first job is to draw out other people and make them interesting, funny, or noteworthy. They ask their guests to contribute new ideas or interesting experiences.

If you're the host, prepare accordingly. Adopt a strategy that creates the event you want. If you want a fun, free-flowing evening, roll out some questions that tap into the easy currents of daily life. Make them open-ended and friendly questions. Ask about the new restaurant, the local football team, or the new Leonardo DiCaprio movie. If you want be sure everyone participates, try throwing out a question with a challenge: Each person has to answer in just one sentence.

> *What's one thing you want everyone to know about you?*
> *If you could transport yourself anywhere in the world right now, go to any country just to eat dinner, where would you go and what would you eat?*

Tagine in Morocco? Pho in Vietnam? Ugali in Kenya? Sounds amazing. What does it taste like? How do they make it? Have you actually been there? Now you've got everyone's mouth watering and imaginations going and a roomful of Anthony Bourdains!

By applying a little "conversation leadership" to get people interacting, you can create an environment that is inclusive, interesting, and dynamic. You can host over dinner or at the beach, at the game or in the office. A few well-placed questions will jump-start a conversation. The more you ask, the more you get. You decide what and how much you want to serve up.

The ingredients for this recipe are readily available and require just a little preparation. Start with a few topics that you know interest everyone. Have a few unexpected subjects you'll mix in as you go. Mix it up with a few lighter, open-ended questions. Listen closely.

Your friend just returned from southern Africa. It was her first time visiting there. She saw the scenery, traveled to Robben Island, and visited Victoria Falls. Your questions, like her travels, reflect different facets of the experience, different levels of awareness.

> *What did you see?*
> *What surprised you?*
> *How did it affect you?*

Daria volunteers at a food bank and feels strongly about the new homeless shelter the city wants to build. Some think it's necessary but others believe it will attract more homeless people. Ask Daria about her experience and what she thinks about this issue that now divides the community.

> *What is our obligation to the homeless?*
> *What about the neighbors?*
> *What do the homeless people you know have to say about this?*

John loves to camp in the Rockies. He once went for two weeks. Alone.

> *Why alone?*
> *Any moose join you for dinner?*
> *What do you think about in such solitude?*

Ask for different levels of experience and awareness. Decide where and how far you want to go. Start with an open-ended question, then ask about examples and encourage stories. Make room for reflection, humor, and emotion.

Supper with Socrates

If you want to play the ultimate question game and challenge friends and family to look for shadows on the wall of what they believe, invite Socrates to supper. A philosopher and a teacher, his famous line of inquiry is as provocative today as it was 2,400 years ago when he turned his questions on his students. You won't have to drink hemlock, but be prepared to challenge people to question their knowledge and their assumptions, to the very core of what they believe.

The Socratic method uses questions to probe from all angles. It pokes at a basic premise or value to force critical thinking and get to the root of an idea. It often answers questions with a question in the search for knowledge or understanding. The Socratic method challenges conventional wisdom. It seeks truth and meaning and holds every answer up to the light to ask "How do we know?"

Having supper with Socrates is not for the faint of heart because Socrates was relentless. He questioned his students' basic assumptions and the very terms of the discussion. He challenged their reasons behind their assumptions. He asked them to consider different viewpoints, then asked where those viewpoints came from and what they were based on. He took nothing for granted.

Socrates might have eagerly joined the conversation at Chris's dinner party when it turned to the political gridlock that afflicts Washington. One guest groused about the glacial pace of government, noting that America will fall further behind if it continues to move so slowly when the world moves so fast. But then another guest observed that "slow" was baked into our system thanks to our Founding Fathers and their checks and balances. Slow protects us from the impetuous or from overreaction. Yes, someone else said, but it also prevents us from keeping up with the competition. Then other questions followed: Does anyone really want "fast"? Is there a difference between "fast" and "efficient"? Why can't we be efficient?

If Socrates had been there, we might still be going. Hang on, he might have said, let's talk about "slow government."

What do you mean by slow? According to whom? Based on what?
Can you give an example? Is that good or bad? Why? Is there a
better way?
What are the pros and cons? And the consequences? Is that
virtuous?
What is virtue, anyway? Better? For whom?
Why did we even ask this question in the first place?

You can see why plenty of people resented the guy, but he sure could keep a conversation going. Despite the dangers, we could invite Socrates to more of our conversations when we're talking about the vexing issues and tough decisions we confront. We might benefit by having a host who challenges us to open our minds and question our most basic assumptions.

Asking for Laughs

Please don't think that every time I gather with family or friends for a meal, it's an interview or interrogation or some deep look into the chasm of the cosmic unknown. Good hosts use questions to have fun, make people laugh, or dive into the ridiculous.

Not long ago, my sister Julie and I were in California, visiting our father and stepmother, Alice. At nearly ninety, Dad still went to his office every day and to the gym twice a week. He looked great and remained eager to enjoy life. Over appetizers, Alice suggested a game my father loved. He'd ask "rating" questions like:

On a scale of one to ten, how important is it to be rich?
What are three qualities you want in a friend?
What are three fun things that matter to you?

Alice told us that she'd asked Dad that last question to figure out what to buy him for Father's Day. His answer: money, clothes and . . . sex. For a moment we didn't quite know what to say. Talking sex with my 90 year-old father was not exactly on my bucket list. Alice, always able to regale a room, leapt on the moment and told us that my father's answers gave her all the gift inspiration she needed. She bought him an expensive shirt and fine chocolates. The designer label shirt covered her on money and clothes. The Godiva chocolate conjured up sex. Lady Godiva rode naked through the streets, after all. We howled at Alice's literary license, recognizing that with age comes freedom to say—and buy—whatever you want.

Then she turned to us and said, "Okay, what three things matter to *you*?" Suddenly we headed in new directions as we listed favorite pastimes and hobbies—long walks in the woods, time on the water, and thoroughly dutiful activities like making a difference and helping others.

Godiva chocolates and sex didn't come up again, fortunately. But having that conversation around Dad's table, in his home of forty years, has become one of those postcard moments, when we shared a laugh and creative memories triggered by a silly question.

A Host of Questions

Whether it's Seinfeld or Socrates joining you for dinner, you can produce an experience your guests will enjoy and remember. They'll relish the discussion as they savor the food. Your hosting, like the meal, takes some preparation. But it's manageable if you tackle the recipe one step at a time.

Start with the most important ingredient, the people. The friends, family, colleagues, students, acquaintances in the group may know one another or they may be strangers, so you should find out whether there are common threads and interests. When I interview, I start by asking: Who is my audience? What do they know? What don't they know? What do they care about? What will they find interesting and funny and why? The more I understand the people in the room, the better I can steer the discussion.

Ask questions, don't answer them. Good hosts participate in the conversation, of course. But they are principally interested in drawing out the others. Their objective is to direct the conversation not dominate it. Pay attention to who's talking and who's not. Direct the questions so everyone gets a chance to talk. But also recognize that some people prefer to listen, so tune in to the signals and listen closely to detect reluctance. Be respectful of the differences.

Mix it up. You can feast on serious topics or small dishes from the lighter side. You can visit a place around the corner or around the world. A good talk-show host alternates topics and moods to keep the conversation moving, varied, and interesting.

Keep watch for the land mines. In my interviews, I go looking for land mines. I like to engage debate head-on. That's my job as a journalist. But interviewing has also taught me that good hosts go looking for buried treasure, too. That's how I discover villages in India and my father's fondest things. But be mindful of topics that at times are best avoided. Politics, religion, and money will inspire some but turn into disasters with others. Know the difference and navigate deliberately.

Go for meaning. Be careful here or you'll be viewed as the humorless professor rather than the cool questioner. You can take just about any topic and look deeper without making it sound heavy or feel like work. Talking baseball? Sure, the standings matter, but on another level, how can this game possibly survive as the national pastime when it takes three hours to play nine innings and the next generation of fans has attention spans that are suited for text messages and six-second videos?

We never invoked Socrates at that dinner party at Chris Schroeder's place. We didn't need to. We were too busy enjoying ourselves, asking and answering entertaining questions, getting to know one another, just having a good time. And examining life along the way.

CHAPTER 12

LESSONS FOR LIFE

Legacy Questions

"SCATTER ME TO THE WIND or take me to Paris."

That was my mother's response when I asked her what she wanted us to do with her after she was gone. For four years she'd been battling her cancer. But when the end came, it came fast. And here we were. She was with us, talking. That's when I broached the subject.

Mom had not made any plans for herself. No plot or memorial, no discussion of where or how. At the point I felt she knew what was coming and was ready for the question, I asked. What do you want us to do with your ashes? She shrugged and offered her one-liner about Paris. I can hear it as vividly today as the moment she uttered it. Mom had visited Paris as a young woman, loved it but had never returned; so it always represented a youthful adventure for her, free from the stresses of life before or after.

I told her I would do what I could. I had visions of going to the Eiffel Tower or stepping behind one of those kiosks on the Rive Gauche, trying to fulfill her dying wish, only to be arrested by a gendarme for littering. It took a while but I delivered. I found a beautiful forest in Provence, overlooking ancient villages and vineyards. I planted some of the ashes at the base of a cedar, took a picture, and reflected on her life. She will be in France forever.

We never had the ultimate deathbed conversation—the final good-bye, the reckoning of a life, the lessons passed along. We didn't do the thank-you-love-you-what-has-it-all-meant-see-you-on-the-other-side discussion. That wasn't her style. I don't think she wanted to face it and I didn't want to force it. In retrospect, that was my mistake. We should have had that conversation. It didn't need to be forced.

> *What are you proudest of in life?*
> *What's one story you'd like me to tell my grandchildren about you?*

How strange that the journalist son failed to string together a few simple questions just to get us started. I think I know what she would have said, but I'll never know for sure. I wish I could have heard her answers in her voice. I just needed to ask.

Seeking Context

I call these *legacy* questions. They ask what we've accomplished or changed and inquire about the lives we've touched. They are questions about meaning, spirituality, lessons learned, gratitude, regrets, people and purpose. Most of us think about questions like these as we move through life—especially toward the end, when we take stock, look back, and think about what it all meant and what difference we made. But legacy questions also ground us along the way. They add meaning to the present and context to the future. By asking them early and often, we take stock of our lives and check our bearings and seek balance.

> *What have I accomplished?*
> *How do I want people to remember me?*

Throughout this book, drawing from my experience as a journalist and the kinds of questions I've asked people over the years, I've examined how to seek answers, chart a course, or pry information out of people who would rather not give it. I've looked at how questions set the stage for creativity and unlock the mysteries of people and the natural world. Legacy questions are different. Whether you ask them of yourself or others, these questions open the door for reflection and resolution. They seek context. They can be existential or spiritual. Whether you are ready to think about a legacy in the literal sense or are merely pondering the meaning of life, legacy questions ask about meaning and gratitude, mistakes and adversity.

You gain perspective from these questions by starting at the end.

Why Didn't I Ask?

My mother was a survivor—as were so many Depression-era kids. Her family lost pretty much everything in the market crash of 1929. Through the early years of the Depression, just as Mom was coming into adolescence, her family was forced to move from place to place. They split up for a time when she and her mother had to move in with relatives in Philadelphia while her father stayed in New York to find work. He finally succeeded, and they reunited, but money remained tight. The jobs were not secure. Her mother went to work too, in a settlement house, but died soon after—of acute appendicitis, most likely—when Mom was just sixteen.

Still, my mother finished public high school in New York City and, egged on by her outspoken aunt, went to college. That was not something a lot of young women did in 1938. College was no escape, however. She was a student when Pearl Harbor shook the planet and pulled America into world war. Shortly after her graduation, her beloved fiancé, an army doctor, diagnosed his own brain tumor. He died before they were to be married. I'm convinced Mom never quite recovered. That Paris trip was a rare escape.

Mom got a job as a social worker, earning $35 a week. That's when she met my dad. They married but were from different worlds. Mom's family had been in America for generations and was educated and established.

Dad's family was first generation, poor, and barely literate. She grew up with role models. He grew up on his own. She was outspoken. He had not yet found himself.

Mom bore the second of her three children in a taxicab as they raced across Manhattan to Lenox Hill Hospital. Lora, born premature, brought something else to the family, Down syndrome. Over the years, her disability became another flashpoint between them. My parents' marriage ended badly, bitterly.

Life was seldom serene and never settled. Mom, always a fighter, battled what she called the "system" to gain education and independent life for Lora. Though she clearly was proud of her kids, she always found something to criticize. But as difficult as she was at times, my mother also was smart and quick and could be wickedly funny. Mom judged everybody with a profane blast that made us wince. "Asshole!" she would shout if the driver ahead of her was turning too slowly. "Idiot," she'd comment if the pharmacist failed to fill the prescription properly.

Mom and I had our own rip-roaring fights. But we could also sit and talk about the world or human nature for hours on end. She had opinions about everything. My youngest sister, Julie, and I were with her at the end. At about 2:30 in the morning, the hospice nurse came in and turned her a bit. Mom opened her eyes and said, "Peace." It was the last word she spoke.

When I went back a couple of days later to thank the hospice staff, I asked the social worker how many people have a meaningful conversation where they come to terms with one another and what they've done in their lives. Do they ask about their lessons learned, resolve some regret, or celebrate their life story?

"Not many," she told me. "Not many."

The Rabbi

Not long after Mom died, and purely coincidentally, the Hospice Foundation of America asked me to host a video for a continuing education course for end-of-life professionals. I didn't hesitate. The course involved interviewing clinicians, hospice workers, physicians, social workers, and spiritual care providers, asking them about research and best practices. They shared their experiences and their stories.

While interviewing these experts, I discovered a common theme. These remarkably caring people, who so clearly see life as a journey and death as an inevitable destination, were uncommonly good listeners and superb questioners. They told of conversations, sometimes with difficult patients or fractured families, that helped people come to terms and grieve, but also to appreciate life and find a narrative—a legacy. Questions served as part of the therapeutic toolkit. Asking people about their fears and concerns, about their quality of life and their accomplishments invited intensely personal and revealing reflection.

One of the most memorable people I met, Rabbi Gary Fink, dealt with the big what and the why questions every day. As the spiritual care adviser for hospice in Montgomery County, Maryland, this soft-spoken man with the gray beard works with people who occupy all parts of the religious spectrum, from those who find comfort in faith to those who reject religion altogether. Still others, he told me, create their own spirituality or approach mortality in a fatalistic way.

Gary Fink never judges. He never rebukes or asks if a patient believes in God. Instead he asks:

What is meaningful to you?

The answers reflect the range of human experience, he explained. Faith. Family. What I did for my school. The work I did with the blind. He asks:

What brings you meaning at this time in your life?

He hears common threads from distinct perspectives: Thanking people. Giving back. Making sure my family will be okay. Knowing that my kids are launched. Pondering what life was all about.

Gary's goal is to get people talking so that they can put their life into perspective. He wants to help them find their sources of meaning. He has his own questions about what and why.

What makes people tick?
Why is the world what it is?

He has thought deeply about the questions people have asked him as they confronted death and tried to make sense of it.

What is going to happen to me physically?
Can I atone for what I've done?
Can I seek reconciliation?

I drove out to Gary Fink's office. It was a low, nondescript brick building that could have been mistaken for a suburban strip mall, except that inside on the walls, there were all sorts of drawings from children to their grandparents, letters of appreciation to the staff, and testimonials to loved ones. I wanted to hear more about the questions people ask, and the questions he asks.

He told me that some of the questions are specific to the moment and have tangible answers.

Can I avoid pain?

Others aren't so easy and ponder the unknowable.

Why is God angry with me?
What will happen to me?
Why is God taking so long?

Gary often replies with a question of his own. "What do you think God might have in mind?" Or, "What thoughts do you have when you ask that question?" A conversation usually follows and becomes a story. "I help people create narratives, each one original, unique, and important," he explained. "And meaning is embedded in all of their narratives."

Gary asks about achievements and failures, people and impact. Sometimes religion is part of the dialogue, sometimes not. He does not preach or judge. He includes the patient's family and friends, inviting them to join the storytelling.

What kinds of things do you think you'll miss the most?
What are the intangible gifts you have now because of your
*   experience with this person?*

The rabbi believes that a properly told life story can capture life's impact and its meaning. But not all stories have happy endings, and not all lives end with clarity or resolution. A question can prompt a reply brimming with guilt or sadness. Anger and sorrow are not uncommon emotions at the end of life, he explains. Gary hears about broken promises, unfulfilled dreams, hurt feelings—all inevitable parts of the story of life. He presses patients and families alike to confront their sadness. He asks without hesitation and encourages dialogue like this:

What kinds of things will you not miss about your mother?

"Mom was just so difficult. She was bitter. She said terrible things."

Was there something you learned from that?

"I vowed never to submit my kids to that. To teach them restraint and patience."

And . . . ?

"If I feel myself losing my temper or getting really angry, I think about what I felt like when my mother turned on me."

What do you do?

"I stop myself."

Does that always work?

"Nearly."

And it's because of your mother?

"Yes."

Has it made you a more careful parent?

"I think so."

Memories of adversity can make a family stronger. In the right context, they can provide comfort. Then, the rabbi says, "you have turned a burden into a blessing."

Facing Failure

Some burdens may seem insurmountable: feelings of acute failure, a sense of a wasted life. But legacy questions can brighten even those dark places. End-of-life expert and author Ken Doka offers proof. A principal contributor to the hospice training video, Doka has worked with all kinds of people, including patients who expressed wrenching regret at the end of life—about their inability to hold a job, stay in school, or provide for themselves or their families. But Doka has found that even these people often can be guided to a more positive, reassuring place. "Sometimes in framing their lives as lessons that others can learn from, there can be meaning," Doka says. "The story may be, 'I made a lot of mistakes. I didn't learn from them, but others can.'"

He describes a young man we'll call Martin, who had been a street hustler since he was a kid. When he had just graduated from high school, Martin went to jail for drug possession. After that, he never could hold a job for long. He was estranged from his entire family, except for a brother, who had asked Martin to be godfather to his nephew. Martin agreed, then failed to show up to the baptism. Furious and disappointed, Martin's brother told him he was "worthless."

Now, still in his twenties, Martin was dying of AIDS. He told Ken he didn't have much to be proud of. No family, no job, no legacy beyond the streets. He was sorry he didn't make it to that baptism. He cared about his nephew.

"What would you say to your nephew?" Ken asked him.

"That I have nothing to give him. That I love him," Martin said.

Ken said, "Look, Martin, you've had some rough times. You've learned a lot of lessons about things you shouldn't do." He asked:

What do you want to pass along to your nephew?

Martin thought for a minute. "Stay in school. Don't do drugs." He spoke softly and paused. Then Martin revealed his secret. He was gay. "I never felt like I belonged while growing up. In my community it was considered a sin."

Ken listened, then asked, "What advice do you have for your nephew?"

"Be yourself."

Ken wrote down Martin's words, went home, and turned them into a letter addressed to Martin's nephew. The next time they visited, he asked, "What do you want me to do with it?"

"Please give it to my brother—for my nephew."

Martin had something to pass along after all.

Ken's questions helped Martin see value in his life story and share it with someone he cared about. Ken believes every life has meaning, though sometimes it takes hard work and persistent questioning to find it. He asks:

How do you put your mistakes in context?
What lessons would you share?
What high points in life would you point to?

End-of-life experts speak in terms of creating a "meaning narrative." They believe this kind of story makes people feel better about life and more positive about themselves. One approach involves a "question protocol" to help patients recall significant personalities, places, activities and experiences in their lives. In one study by Harvey Chochinov and others, printed in the August 20, 2005, issue of *Journal of Clinical Oncology*, the researchers asked terminally ill patients to describe when they felt most alive, to recount their most important roles and accomplishments, and to share their hopes and dreams for their loved ones. The researchers edited the responses into a "generativity document" to be given to a family member or friend. When the patients read their document, two-thirds reported a "heightened sense of meaning." Nearly half said their will to live had increased. "Getting down on paper what I thought was a dull, boring life really opened my eyes to how much I really have done," a forty-nine-year-old woman said.

In Search of Meaning

Questions of death lead to questions of life. One of the most moving assignments I had when I worked at CNN involved Oregon's "Death with Dignity" law. The provision permitted people diagnosed with a terminal illness and less than six months to live to obtain a prescription that would end their lives if they decided that's how they wanted to die. My story revolved around Greg Yaden, a fifty-nine-year-old Oregon man who was dying of leukemia.

The day before I met Greg, he had received a blood transfusion to replenish his failing white blood cells. We met at his front door. He offered a firm handshake and he spoke in a clear voice. Though he looked pale, his stride was sure and strong. He'd planned an ambitious day for us and he was anxious to begin. With camera crew in tow, we fished for trout at a stream not far from his home, had a beer at his favorite bar, and then sat in his backyard for the interview.

He told me he had never finished college, had worked a variety of jobs around the country, and had been married twice. He was now living with his girlfriend, Missy. The two had met ten years before, when he was working in California. They had moved together to Oregon, where they both had the "freedom to roam."

Greg had been traveling on business when he felt pain while walking through the airport. Arthritis, maybe, he thought. Then one day he got dizzy just walking to the store. His head felt like it would explode. He went to the doctor, who ordered tests. They came back with the deadly diagnosis. Intensive chemo wasn't enough; he would also need a stem cell transplant. Greg's doctor's conducted an exhaustive search for a compatible donor, which included his brother, without success. Between the chemo and the waiting, it was a rough ride. Greg finally made a decision. "Gang, here's what I'm thinking," he told the doctors. "The anxiety is getting a little rough on me. Sitting by the phone waiting and waiting and waiting and getting my hopes up. I really thank you so much for searching the world, but let's just move on and let's look at having a good quality of life." He wanted the freedom to roam. That's how he lived and it's how he wanted to die.

Greg signed up for a drug cocktail that would end his life on his own terms, if he chose. It wasn't about pain or hastening the end, he told me. It was about having control.

What are the high points of your life?

Greg talked about the jobs he'd had, the places he'd been, and the people he knew. Meeting Missy was a high point. And despite the divorces, he was close to his extended family. "I'm a brand-new grandpa, so I'm passing the torch," he said.

What do you want to say to that grandson of yours?

"Seize life," Yaden responded instantly. "Just go get her. Have fun. Be good. Be a good human being and go have fun. Don't hurt anybody else. Be good. If you want to do something, just go do it." He told me he had narrowed down and written his rules to live by: "Don't be afraid of failure. Be a kind human being."

I will never forget this ordinary man who was so thoughtful, courageous, and composed. He had never been in politics and wasn't an advocate, but he was devoting his waning energy, and some of his precious remaining time, to advocate for this law and share this story with me. He needed to make a point, he said. He wanted people to know about control and dignity. And about the journey. "I am a great advocate of choice," Greg told me. "Oregon and the voters have given me the opportunity to end my life with some control and dignity. I'm in good company because death is inevitable for all of us. That's pretty comforting." This last mission—standing up for a belief—helped lend his life greater meaning. Greg wanted to talk. He had a lot to say. All I had to do was ask.

Greg died two months after I visited. He didn't need the medicine.

Asking for Life

We do not need to wait for the deathbed moment to ask about the meaning of our lives. Legacy questions travel with us. If we have the courage to ask them, they help us get our bearings and write our story. If we listen closely to our answers—even if they are not clear or uncomplicated—we gain perspective. As I was working on this book, my daughter shared an email she'd received from her friend, Jen. At twenty-five, Jen had led a pretty darn interesting life. She had traveled the world, gotten a terrific education, and had more options in life than most. But she had paused to ask about the meaning and the priorities of her options, where they would take her, and what she would get out of them. Her questions would have made Gary Fink, Ken Doka, and Greg Yaden proud.

> *What are we supposed to do?*
> *Should we all have jobs that mean everything to us?*
> *That consume us?*
> *There are wonderful occupations and careers out there that offer*
> *   rewarding and fascinating experiences. But is that the dream?*
> *What else is there to devote one's life to?*
> *What do we give most to and receive most from?*
> *Relationships?*
> *Is a relationship supposed to be your whole life?*
> *What do you escape to when you're not at work?*
> *A cause or a mission?*
> *Try to save the world?*

Call it the indulgence of youth, but I know a lot of forty- and fifty- and sixty-year-olds who ask—or should ask—variations on these questions. Jen just started early. Even if she never comes up with definitive answers, she will appreciate and consider her choices more thoughtfully for continuing to ask.

Legacy questions serve as signposts.

What are you proudest of?
What is the most important life lesson you have learned?
What is your unfinished business?
What is your story?

I never got a chance to ask my mother these questions. Not that her feelings were much of a secret. She was never short of opinions. But I should have asked; she would have answered. She would have said she wanted to be remembered not for being nice but for having principles. She believed the world needs more fierce advocates who fight for what's right. Mom was proudest of Lora, who despite her Down syndrome defied the odds and just about everyone's expectations. Mom spoke often about the moment, soon after Lora's birth, when she threw the doctor out of the room. He had said he was sorry she had given birth to a "mongoloid" child and offered to contact an institution that would put her away.

My sister Lora has lived semi-independently for nearly forty years. She has traveled on her own, participated in the Special Olympics, and become adept at caning chairs and making pottery. Her work adorns our home. She talks to her dad every week. She still misses her mother.

Lora will read this story, and she will ask me a whole lot of questions.

CHAPTER 13

I'M GLAD I ASKED

I EMBARKED ON THIS project to discover a better and more disciplined way to ask questions. I wanted to find out if questioning could be organized around specific objectives and how the types of questions we ask affect how we listen. Though I had asked questions all my life as a journalist and interviewer, I never thought of them as "strategic" or "creative" or "empathetic." I didn't build inquiry around outcomes. But as I talked to close to 100 people for this book, curious souls skilled at turning questions into discovery and results, I became convinced that a "taxonomy" of questions, each with its own approach and compelling benefits, could serve as a useful way to think about what and how we ask. I don't pretend that my way of approaching questions is definitive; some of the best inquiry is generated by random curiosity. But by understanding what we're asking, how we listen, and when we should ask more, we can become better questioners with tangible results to show for it.

Still, we must appreciate that questions are not a blank check. There *is* such a thing as a stupid question. I've heard plenty of them over the years. Stupid questions reveal willful ignorance, laziness, or a painful lack of preparation. There are also hurtful questions that humiliate or open old wounds. Gratuitously hostile questions—meant to embarrass or pick a fight—can poison a conversation. Inappropriately personal queries can get you in trouble. Self-serving questions, where someone asks a question just to show off how much he or she really knows, turn off everyone else.

Cultural sensitivities vary widely; one person's question may be another's insult. Some cultures defer to age and authority or view public questioning as inappropriate or disrespectful.

A few years ago, while teaching a university class in China, I employed what I thought was some good, provocative Socratic questioning about what the United States and China were up to in the world and how the students perceived the competition. I challenged the students to share their opinions, define their terms, and support their views. A Chinese student leaned over to one of the Americans in the room and asked, "What is he doing, trying to get us to fight?" This was unfamiliar, uncomfortable territory for these students and my questions landed with a thud.

In some societies, questions are viewed as an outright threat. Repressive regimes know they cannot stand up to scrutiny or challenge. Thought dictatorships reject accountability and suppress curiosity.

A "Letter from Pyongyang" in the *Washington Post* caught my eye. Entitled "Virtual Reality Inside North Korea," the article by Anna Fifield told the story of her tour of a North Korean hospital with a group of reporters. A secretive, brutally repressive state, North Korea wanted to show off healthcare in the communist paradise. The tour was surreal. Fifield saw "decades-old" incubators in the maternity ward and a lab stocked with "a museum exhibit of scientific instruments." She asked one of the doctors who was assigned to the group whether international sanctions "limited your ability to get the technology you need to do your work."

Sanctions had caused suffering, came the answer, but "Great Leader Marshal Kim Jong-un taught us to learn about technology and science so we have the ability to develop by ourselves."

Later in the tour, Fifield asked if the doctor had access to the internet. He went to a nearby building to go online three or four times a week, he replied. Had he been online this past week? "No, no times this week."

As they passed a CT scanner, Fifield asked if they could turn it on so she could see it work. The response: "Why? Do you have a serious health problem?"

"You ask too many questions," Fifield's government minder told her. "It's a little hard to work with you."

In North Korea, there's no point and little future in asking.

In vibrant societies, however, we want our next generation of questioners to be better than the last. Indeed, the people I spoke with for this book know that the ability to ask is directly connected to our ability to invent and innovate, to push boundaries and pose the big questions that confront us as a society. Some have dedicated themselves to teaching young people and helping future generations understand the power and poetry of questions. Three such individuals stood out for their commitment to the future.

The Justice of Citizenship

Justice Sandra Day O'Connor asked some of the biggest questions confronting America during her twenty-five years on the United States Supreme Court. Though she had been retired for several years, she still kept an office deep inside the massive neoclassical building. Justice O'Connor was in her eighties. A cane leaned against her desk. But her voice was strong and clear as she rose without effort to greet me.

We weren't there to discuss her opinions in some of the most significant cases in American history—not *Bush v. Gore*, when the Court (with her crucial vote) picked a president; nor *Planned Parenthood v. Casey*, when she sided with the liberal justices upholding *Roe v. Wade*. "I don't look back," she told me definitively. "That's for a historian or a book writer. I did the best I could and that's that."

We were there to talk instead about her initiative to teach young people about the important questions of government and citizenship. Sitting in her cavernous office, wrapped with shelves heavy with books on law and government, it was impossible not to feel the weight of history and the great debates that had defined America. The American experience, Justice O'Connor explained, was built on defining questions.

Are we going to be a nation?
If so, what form of government are we going to choose?
And how will the people be part of resolving it?

On July 2, 1776, the Second Continental Congress voted to declare independence from Great Britain and its tyrannical king. The next day John Adams, in one of his famous letters to his wife, Abigail, wrote, "Yesterday, the greatest question was decided, which ever was debated in America, and a greater, perhaps, never was nor will be decided among men." From there, a nation of ideas evolved.

Some 240 years later, O'Connor was worried. We were losing our sense of history, civics, and our understanding of these big questions, she feared. Our schools were failing us. As a parent, years earlier, she had been struck by how little time her children and their friends spent studying how government worked. It had only gotten worse. She felt young people urgently needed to learn what "citizens have to do and decide" if they were to participate in the world around them.

The words hit me hard in this place, especially as I considered the polarizing, paralyzing debate that passed for political discourse outside. Benjamin Franklin is often credited with saying, "It is the first responsibility of every citizen to question authority." But citizens need to know whom to question and how, if they are to do it effectively.

Motivated by the conviction that citizens must understand the basics of government if they are to question and change it, O'Connor started iCivics, an online teaching tool that uses games and interactive exercises to help young people learn how government works and how they can be part of the process. At the time we spoke, more than 100,000 teachers and 3 million students had visited iCivics, playing its educational video games more than 10 million times.

O'Connor wanted future generations to understand and to engage America's foundational questions:

What is the role of government?
How do we balance individual liberty with social responsibility?
What does responsible citizenship entail?

Justice O'Connor seemed as proud of her iCivics initiative as her years on the bench. Hers was an astonishing career. She broke virtually every barrier that got in her way. She made history in her own right as the first woman to serve on the Supreme Court. But helping young people appreciate the American experiment and what it asks of them as citizens was a mission that lit her up.

"I think we've achieved something," she told me modestly.

Ask to Lead

Debbie Bial is passionate in her belief that young people who ask the next generation's questions will be its leaders. Debbie founded and runs The Posse Foundation, an organization that identifies extraordinary high school students based on their talents and leadership potential. Mostly from inner cities, the "Posse scholars" are paired with colleges and universities that provide full tuition. The groups of students that go to these schools are known as Posses. They are the most engaged, motivated, and diverse kids you could ever meet. When they get to campus, many take on leadership roles or start new student organizations. Most are the first in their families to go to college. I have worked with Posse scholars for years and served on the Posse Board. I'm a true believer.

The Posse recruitment and selection process is structured around stimulating and often intensely reflective questions. Debbie builds communication skills and leadership qualities into the scholars' experience by constantly asking them about themselves and the world around them. At student gatherings, board meetings, and staff retreats, Debbie uses question exercises as "catalysts for dialogue." She shows participants pictures or news stories about a topic that cuts close to home—race, class, climate, the election—and asks:

When you think about this, how does it affect or influence your
*   everyday life?*
How does it affect your job?
Where are you in this story?

She asks a roomful of people to form two lines facing each other. Everyone gets a question and has sixty seconds to answer.

What labels do you use to describe yourself, or do you use no labels?
Are your labels different from labels others use?
What's the greatest risk you've ever taken?

She asks a group to sit in a circle.

What's the hardest thing you've ever experienced?
If you were to sit down for lunch with your nineteen-year-old self,
*   who would you see?*
What percentage of you is your dark side?

"We create a structured framework around the question," Debbie explained, in order to build relationships, provoke conversation, develop leadership, and create bridges between communities. At a time of increasing diversity in America, and as everything seems to get more complex, Debbie argues that leadership starts with an ability to ask and to listen, to bridge differences and build community. She's betting the future on it.

"The question as a tool is the core of everything we do," she says.

Poems of Humanity

David Isay, like Debbie Bial and Sandra Day O'Connor, is also investing in the future. Isay is creator of StoryCorps, a project that millions of listeners hear on podcasts, NPR, and online. StoryCorps invites ordinary citizens to interview one another. Parents, children, husbands, wives, friends, and partners produce remarkable conversations that evoke a rich and enduring spoken mosaic of American life. StoryCorps declares that its mission is to "preserve and share humanity's stories in order to build connections between people and create a more just and compassionate world."

Forty-minute interviews get edited to three minutes. Each interview is intensely personal in its own way: A mother forgives the man who murdered her son and says she hopes to see him graduate from college; a military veteran asks his wife, "What made you stick around?" as he wrestled with rage and alcohol driven by his post-traumatic stress disorder (PTSD); a man with Down syndrome answers his mother's questions about growing up with a curse he now calls a gift.

The appointment with a microphone, Isay told me, creates time and license to ask about subjects that normally get buried or dismissed. Story-Corps offers a list of "Great Questions" to get the conversations started.

What was the happiest moment of your life?
Was there a time when you didn't like me?
What makes us such good friends?

StoryCorps interviews are archived at the American Folklife Center at the Library of Congress, allowing participants to leave a legacy for future generations.

Isay told me that many of these conversations become "poems of humanity." He's right. Each story speaks in its distinct cadence, offering a unique journey to an individual's life story. The poetry happens because someone asked.

Always Asking

It was inspiring to hear from these people who work so hard to advance the culture of curiosity. It is a message educators try to convey to students every chance we get: A successful education is one that only gets you started. It's not the questions you've answered, but the ones you have yet to ask that will lead to discovery, ensure your place in the world, and help you succeed at a time of rapid change.

I tried to do my part over the years and when my kids were young, though I encountered some predictable resistance. I had a reputation for mealtime interviewing. I asked about school, homework, sports, friends, weekend plans—all the activities that kids are into and parents want to know about. I thought I was being a good dad, projecting my interest in my kids and their friends, encouraging them to tell stories and share with the family. But my questions could cause fifteen-year-old eyes to roll. My son would say, "Dad, it's dinnertime. Stop being a reporter." I defended myself, of course, and asked again.

> *What was one new thing you learned in school today?*
> *If you could visit any time and place in history, where would you go?*
> *What's the book about?*
> *Who is your favorite teacher? Why?*
> *Who do you confide in when you are confused?*

My son Chris recalled that "as kids, we used to joke that Dad could ask the same questions in thirty different ways."

As the kids got older, my questions grew up too.

> *Does money matter?*
> *How much is too much?*
> *Is there something you believe in so strongly that you would give your life for it?*
> *How do you know if you have had a successful life?*

While my household interviewing became a family joke, my kids did answer my questions most of the time. Now that they are grown, they still trot out the "Dad's playing reporter" line when it fits, and we all have a good laugh. Sure, I overdid it at times, and I realize a fine line exists between asking enough and asking too much, between showing interest and prying. That's why listening is so important. It not only helps you learn, it also helps you shut up. But I'm glad I asked all those questions. My curiosity in their lives reflected both my interest in their present and my investment in their future. I'm pretty sure they'll grill their kids someday, too.

––––––––––

My life has been enriched at every stage by the opportunities I've had to question. I have been invited into people's lives and adventures, taken on fascinating journeys because I've had license to ask more. Different places and different audiences have afforded distinct opportunities.

For years, I hosted CNN's Sunday morning talk show. Each week, I questioned prominent people and dove into the issues, triumphs, setbacks, and controversies that had made headlines. I questioned the Israeli prime minister in the midst of crisis. I spoke with the CIA director as he walked me around the agency to show a slice of how they tracked the world. I asked medical experts about the latest global health crisis. It was the hard news, the front page of cable news, driven by questions that explained the story.

At The George Washington University, I started the *Conversation Series*, a more informal discussion with public figures in front of a live audience. My questions there revolved around the guests' accomplishments, their views of public life and their explanations for the positions they took. With my next-generation crowd in mind, I asked how my guests got started and what they recommended to young people who wanted to make their mark. I came to think of these interviews as conversations with the future.

On NPR, I had the pleasure occasionally to host the Diane Rehm Show. Diane captained her very smart show for more than thirty-five years. Her story is richly ironic. Growing up in Washington DC in an Arab household, Diane was not allowed to question her parents or much else in her life. Such behavior was considered disrespectful. Yet she became one of the great interviewers, demonstrating that radio is a magical and intimate medium. Sitting in for Diane, I had a chance to interview a fabulous range of people, from bestselling authors like Jane Goodall and Nicholas Kristof, to experts too obscure for cable TV but ideally suited to insightful conversation on public radio. The questions here embraced complexity.

I will always be grateful to the people over the years who answered my questions, humoring my ignorance, feeding my curiosity, allowing me to hold them to account. They were my tour guides through ideas, history, and great human events that I never would have experienced otherwise. They told compelling stories as they went. I could ask anything, go anywhere.

But for all my experience asking and listening, I didn't appreciate how much more there was to learn about the discipline of inquiry until I tackled this book. The people who talked to me patiently explained how they worked, how they framed their questions, and what they listened for. Each one of them showed me how asking more, in a more disciplined way, could lead to tangible results and deeper understanding. They, too, used their questions to invest in the future.

Simone, my student whose experience encouraged me to launch this project, learned her family secret because she had an assignment to ask. She realized a deeper relationship with her father as a result.

Barry Spodak put his troubled human puzzles together by taking time to slowly build bridges. His work helped the people trying to keep us safe.

Jim Davis built his business by asking for team players, listening for "we" not "I." His company, New Balance, is global but still makes shoes in America.

Rick Leach enlisted people to take on the daunting challenge of feeding the world by asking them to share a vision: Hunger is a solvable problem.

Tony Fauci, who knew his quest would never end, pushed the bounds of science to take on disease. His questions drove research that saved lives.

Ed Bernero and Gavin Newsom used questions to push people into an imagined reality where they could think differently and imagine a different world.

Terry Gross and Betty Pristera asked people to reveal the essence of themselves. They walked in other people's shoes and discovered new places as a result.

Anderson Cooper and Jorge Ramos demanded explanation. They confronted their adversaries with the most challenging questions so that everyone could see and judge.

Chris Schroeder's recipe for dinnertime conversation and brilliant entertaining questions forged new ideas and friendships.

General Colin Powell started with an "estimate of the situation" and used strategic questioning to determine whether the situation was worthy of the investment. He saw that strategic questions must challenge conventional wisdom and groupthink.

Nurse practitioner Teresa Gardner and roofer Al Darby became experts in asking, "What's wrong?" They knew they couldn't fix a problem if they couldn't identify its source.

Rabbi Gary Fink answered a question with a question, prompting a conversation that would provide comfort and meaning at life's most challenging time.

Profane and Profound

Although the roadmap to inquiry I've drawn can help us navigate with a more deliberate eye, there are always alternate routes—scenic drives that take us to unexpected destinations. Questions that spring from pure curiosity can turn into gold. Unplanned detours can lead to serendipity, as I also found during the interviews for this book. One such conversation left me speechless, and I will end by sharing it with you.

As I was talking with Dr. Anthony Fauci at the National Institutes of Health about scientific inquiry and how it could be useful to nonscientists, something was gnawing at me. In his discussion about research in the early days of AIDS, Fauci spoke about the work, about the research and the discoveries, about patients and process. His observations were fascinating, and not without feeling. But he sounded, well, like a scientist—captivated by his research and his breakthroughs and setbacks. Yet Fauci had a perspective almost no one could imagine and I wondered: What was it like for him in those days, caught in the middle of the colliding worlds of medicine, culture, and politics, to see such human suffering? I recalled the headlines from the time, which revealed igno-rance, fear and bigotry. I interrupted our science discussion to ask:

Did you ever wonder how can this be happening out there and ask
yourself, can I make them see what I am seeing?

Suddenly, this man of science fell silent. His lips trembled and his eyes filled with tears. Finally he spoke. "I am actually laughing and crying at the same time," he said. "I have a lot of suppressed feelings from back then."

He paused and gathered himself. And then he slowly erupted.

"The answer to your question is yes. There was a lot of, you know, 'What the fuck is going on here?'"

Another pause.

"It was not easy when you see everybody die. So I need to say this in a way without getting more emotional about it. There were multiple years, from 1981 to 1986, where you wanted to keep a positive outlook. But everybody died. Everybody died . . ."

He wiped his tears.

"That was probably one of the things that gave me the phenomenal energy to get solutions. People say, 'How come you didn't burn out? You know, thirty-three years and you kept on doing your work for seventeen, eighteen hours a day.' It was that kind of realization that this was an enormous problem."

He leaned forward and spoke deliberately, emphatically.

"And the thing that was, I guess, a little bit different was there was something about—and I want to make sure I say it accurately—there was something about the young gay population that was, I think, par-ticularly tragic. Because most of the time—and you never made judg-ments about your patients and their personality—but in general, as a demographic group, they were gentle, artistic, kind. There were very few assholes among them. There were a lot of good, gentle people who were scared shitless. And for those years, they came in and there really wasn't a lot you could do for them . . .

"It was very painful and very frustrating, and the thing that got me to have this response is—you are right, there was a lot of bullshit going on in the outside. Not giving them insurance, throwing them out of their houses. And you think what a shit world we live in.

"It is interesting that you ask that question," he said to me. "I have not had an emotional response to this in twenty-five years."

Perhaps I looked away at that moment.

"Sorry. No," he said. "It's fine and it's cathartic."

Fauci's comments sprang from his gut, raw and profane, triggered by a single question that had nothing to do with the scientific method. He shared his passion. He took me to the roots of his emotions and displayed his rage and his frustration and his humanity. I felt privileged to have experienced the intensity of this remarkable man. It was like stepping to the edge of a volcano and peering over it to see the molten lava and feel the heat.

This book is dedicated to the curiosity and passion in us all. Questions are humanity's unique attribute. They are our investment in ourselves and in the future. When we ask more, we open our minds and challenge others to open theirs. We organize our thoughts so we can tackle big ideas and probe with precision. We learn and lead and discover.

Questions are our way to connect with other human beings. I believe that inquiry, not imitation, is the sincerest form of flattery. Ask a good question and you convey interest. Slow down, listen closely, and ask more and you engage at a deeper level. You show that you care. You generate trust. You empathize and you bridge differences. You become a better friend, colleague, innovator, citizen, leader, or family member. You shape the future.

You can't ask for more than that.

QUESTION GUIDE

DIAGNOSTIC QUESTIONS

Before you can fix a problem, you need to know what it is. Get it right, and you're on your way. Get it wrong and you face the consequences, and they can be costly. These questions help identify a problem with precision, on several levels, separating the symptoms from the disease. Start broad, zero in. Describe, compare, and quantify. Listen for detail and patterns.

Open-Ended Problem Questions:

What's going on here?
What's the matter?

The first step is to ask what's wrong. Using broad, open-ended questions, ask for a description of the problem—what it looks, sounds and feels like. Ask where it manifests itself, when, and in what ways. Ask about what seems to make the problem better or worse. These are present-tense questions designed to get a full and accurate description of the problem from all angles.

History Taking: When did this problem begin? How has it changed? How does it compare? History repeats itself. Learn from it. Look for comparisons, parallels, patterns. Ask about previous experience with the problem—when it was first detected, how it's changed over time, what's been done to address it in the past. Ask whether it's gotten worse and in what ways. Ask what's been tried in the past and with what effect. Compare then and now. Use the past to inform the present. These questions use history to seek detail to understand what happened, under what conditions, and with what result.

The Mystery: What are we missing? Now that you know the present and the past, drill deeper and ask what don't we know. What else could be at work here to cause the problem? Is there a dirty little secret, a hidden agenda, a mistake, or an unintended action that has made the situation worse? Did a shortcut become a short circuit? These are beneath-the-surface questions that ask about miscues, mistakes, and missed signals.

Verification Questions: Are you sure? How do you know? Can you take this information to the bank? Once you have a diagnosis, you want to be sure it's right. Double-check the sources and know where the information comes from. Determine whether the people you're relying on have an agenda or an ax to grind. What are their qualifications? What's their track record? Ask for an explanation about their process and what their conclusion is based on. Consider a second opinion. These are the corroborating questions that help you understand the basis of the diagnosis and give you confidence that it is correct. Now you can deal with it.

Ask Again: In the medical field, clinicians and researchers have created a number of techniques to get patients talking and to describe their condition in detail. By connecting symptoms and patterns to knowledge and experience, a medical professional will be able to diagnose the problem or will order up the right tests to take the next step toward a diagnosis. You can adapt this pattern of questioning—describe, compare, quantify, connect—to virtually any situation where you are trying to determine what's wrong and why. Ask clearly and persistently, and ask more than once.

Listen: In asking diagnostic questions, listen closely to words used to describe the problem and its symptoms. Key in to details about where and when the problem occurs, and actions that connect to it or seem to cause it. Listen for patterns. Listen for detail and for the connection between the problem and actions that seem to make it better or worse.

Try: Have a conversation with a family member who is not feeling well. Start with open-ended questions and then get more specific. Where does it hurt? Can you quantify it, rate it on a scale of one to ten? Does anything you do make it better? Worse? How does the discomfort compare to previous instances when you felt like this? If you can stay focused and keep asking, you will find it easier to extend your attention span and drill down to determine the cause of a problem.

STRATEGIC QUESTIONS

You're about to make a major decision that will affect your life, your business, or your community. You're considering a move, and it requires a big investment of time, resources, and energy. Your future is on the line. Strategic questions zoom out and look at the big picture. They ask about long-term goals, interests, and priorities. They consider alternatives, consequences, and risks. These questions sharpen the focus on the larger objective, the higher calling, and clarify what it will take to get there.

The Big Question:

What are you trying to do? Why?
What difference will it make?

Start at 20,000 feet. The Oxford Dictionary defines strategic as "relating to the identification of long-term or overall aims and interests and the means of achieving them." Ask whether everyone is even ready to think strategically. Ask about the mission. What's in play, what's at stake, and what is the strategic, long-range purpose or objective?

Cost and Consequence: How will you achieve your objective? What will it cost? What are the downsides? Now that you've defined the goals, ask about their consequences. How will they affect the business, the bottom line, the organizational profile, personal happiness, or real-world activities? Get specific. What's the cost? Ask how your plan and its component pieces translate strategic objectives into metrics and outcomes based on the time, resources, and objectives. Ask who you would help if you succeeded.

Trade-offs: What's the downside? What are the risks? What are you not thinking about? Trade-offs are built into any big decision: You can make more money but will have less free time; you can fix the bottom line but will have to lay off workers; you can liberate a country but will cause damage and death. Trade-off questions openly, sometimes defiantly, ask about risk and downsides. They ask people to calculate when there are no formulas. These are questions that challenge groupthink, conventional wisdom, and your own biases. Think of them as circuit breakers in strategic questioning.

Alternatives: What are your options? Is there another way? Ask about options that can achieve the same outcome. Keeping your strategic objective constant, ask whether there are different tactics that can lower the cost or raise the prospects for success. These questions take the trade-offs and the risks and ask how they can be minimized by applying different approaches and timelines.

Define Success: How will you know when you get there? What will success look like? How will you measure it? Any good military commander relentlessly asks about the "end state": what "mission accomplished" really looks like. Ask what success means and what it will take to get there. Be sure answers are clear, commonly understood, and widely shared. These questions are the cornerstone of strategic thinking. They clarify destination and set expectations. They help navigate, set sights, and articulate a vision.

Listen: Invite questions from a wide range of perspectives. Listen closely for unexpected obstacles or unexplored risk. Listen for scenarios that call for additional consideration. Listen for gratuitous compliments or qualified agreement that conceal deeper problems or concerns. Listen for indications that people don't understand the purpose, the mission, or the goal. That will help you determine whether it's just the message that needs to be sharpened or whether the strategy itself needs to be rethought.

Try: Engage a group about your big idea. Explain the reasoning behind it. Then ask everyone to challenge you, your logic, and your tactics. Answer questions with more questions. Limit your comments and questions to 30 percent of the meeting, so others are speaking and you are listening 70 percent of the time.

EMPATHY QUESTIONS

Empathetic questions go for feeling. They seek deeper, more emotional answers to explore what makes people tick, think, fear, and feel. They help people reveal themselves to others—and sometimes to themselves. These questions are best accessed through "perspective-taking" when the questioner imagines the world from the other person's point of view. Empathy contributes to more compassionate and more effective questioning and more reflective responses.

Origins: What's going on? How are you feeling? These big, open-ended questions are ridiculously simple, but asked intentionally and accompanied by good listening, they grant running room and license. They invite people to open up and they drive a conversation that, with good follow-up questions, can become deeply revealing and rewarding.

Brick by Brick: Rather than throwing a big question at someone and expecting a big answer, which can be overwhelming, use a methodical step-by-step approach that explores detail and pattern. The questions should be pursued deliberately and with purpose to break the issue down while heading toward a destination. Ask in sequence and for increasing detail. What was your family like? Did you have dinner together? What did you talk about? What did you argue about? What made you laugh?

Appreciative Inquiry: What are the most significant things you've done? What's the best part of your job? These questions frame the subject in a positive direction so that a constructive framework can be noted and built. The question "appreciates" the anticipated response, which can connect to other positive thoughts and ideas. Follow up or ask about something positive and you might take the conversation in an entirely different direction.

Empathic listening is riveted to words, tone, pacing, pauses, and expressions. But it also involves facial expressions and affect. What you hear and see helps you read the conversation and connect with your next question.

Intimate Distance: How does this make you feel? I'm not judging, I'm just listening. Be intimate enough to ask, distant enough to maintain perspective. If you are going to engage emotions, it's often best to embrace them without getting caught up in them.

Listen: What are indicators that someone is opening up or sharing something intensely private? Listen for words that convey intense feeling or suggest stress, fear, insecurity, a hidden piece of the past or, on the positive side, deep gratitude, happiness, or tranquility. Listen for clues about the origins of these feelings. Pay special attention to whether this information is being offered willingly or hesitantly, for the first time or with trepidation and use these cues as indicators to keep going or back off. Listen especially hard for anything that might require more expertise than you bring to the conversation.

Try: Conduct a thirty-minute "interview" where the only thing you do is ask questions of the other person. Keep your questions brief and to the point—a single sentence should do it most of the time. Have a starting point—the person's time in the military or in college or growing up in a small town. Listen and follow up with another question. Do not make comments or observations. There are two words you may not use in your questions: "I" and "me." This discussion is exclusively focused on the other person. See if you can keep it there.

BRIDGING QUESTIONS

Bridging questions connect with people who are wary, reluctant, hostile, distant, or menacing. These questions begin by getting people talking, in hopes of establishing rapport, perhaps even trust. These questions may work subtly and over time. They are framed to encourage and reinforce. They are deliberate, and at times manipulative. They can be questions without question marks.

The Comforter: I like your shoes. Where did you get them? You're a Giants fan—what do you think of the season so far? Start out by establishing a rapport. Hit the pleasure center in the person's brain by making reference to an interest you share or an expertise you acknowledge in the other person. Express respect and validate where appropriate. Start with questions that may have nothing to do with the topic at hand. Then work your way to the harder questions.

The Reward: That's interesting. I never thought of it that way before. Affirm or express the other person's point to validate and encourage further conversation. Use a short affirming phrase that does not actually endorse the other person's behavior or belief. *A lot of people feel that way*. People given a reward will often unconsciously return the favor. Rewarding what someone just said may encourage more information or discussion.

The Question Without a Question Mark: Tell me more. Explain that to me. These "questions without question marks" turn a question into a request. Saying "tell me more" sends a signal of acknowledgment and validation because you have, in essence, accepted the predicate of what that person just said. You want to learn more. Wary people may feel isolated and unappreciated. Expressing interest and requesting explanation can frame the issue as legitimate rather than as a point of contention or accusation.

The Echo: It was SHOCKING? You fed TWO HUNDRED people? You say he HUMILIATED you? These questions are exclamation points and question marks rolled into one. They are a product of careful listening. They echo a single word or phrase you just heard that suggests a significant observation or experience. They almost always prompt the person to whom they are directed to pause, go deeper, and explain further. If you hear something surprising, significant or new, or if you hear a word that holds surprise or emotion, echo it back, without comment or embellishment.

The Reinforcer: Is this what we're talking about? Is this what you mean? Reinforcing questions seek to validate and draw out. In posing the question, you acknowledge the other person's stated or unstated sentiments. If your child says, "It's not fair that my brother gets a bigger allowance," a reinforcing questioner would not ask, "Is that why you stole the money?" Instead, the questioner might say, "You think we favor your brother. Is that what we're talking about? Experts say you're more likely to get more of a response and an accurate statement of the facts (even a confession) with this technique.

Listen: Because bridging questions reach across a chasm of suspicion, listen for information or for references that offer clues as to why someone is angry, alienated, or aggrieved. Listen for detail, description, and mood. Listen for expressions of wariness, blame, references to others, attributes and expressions of power or menace. Listen for shards of information you can build on, one small piece at a time. That's how you build the bridge.

Try: Put together a list of ten questions you would ask a person who is distant or wary. Design your questions purely to get the person talking. Ask about the weather, things you observe, the music in the distance, anything that might represent a common thread. Start with open-ended questions. How are you doing? What's going on? Be prepared to listen and make eye contact. Find someone to ask—your rebellious teen, a resentful cousin or the homeless lady you walk past every day. Remember, you're aiming for conversation, not for miracles. You build this bridge one question and one answer at a time.

CONFRONTATIONAL QUESTIONS

Confrontational questions are in-your-face questions. They accuse. They call to account. Ask these questions when someone has done something wrong. Confrontational questions may not produce a willing response, but they establish a record and they force an issue. They make a point, often publicly.

The Facts: Were you there when this went down? Did you say this? Sometimes you start with these inquiries, sometimes you circle around to them, but these are the questions that establish the connection between the person you're questioning and the activity at hand. They may be simple yes-or-no questions. They confront your adversary with an event, an act, with words or facts, and they ask about this person's connection to them. You probably already know the answer because often it is public knowledge.

The Accusation: Did you do it? Did you mean it? Why didn't you *stop* it? Take the allegation, add a question mark, and throw it at the accused. This question demands a response—a denial, an admission, or an obvious dodge. It asks explicitly about the wrongdoing you are alleging. The question is intended to put the accused on the defensive. It frames the confrontation.

The Denial: Do you own a red convertible? Did you drive that car on the day in question? Did you stop for gasoline? Since denial, quasi-denial, or obfuscation is often the first response, you must anticipate a nonanswer and be prepared to come back at it in persistent ways. Take the incident apart piece by piece. Ask about the evidence, the timeline, eyewitness reports, the person's own words, or the historical record. Use them to reveal inconsistency or hypocrisy, lies or misbehavior. These questions can force a response, make a point, or simply call out your adversary.

For the Record: When are you going to tell the staff about the layoffs? Will you agree to testify publicly? Why did you lie? Sometimes the best confrontational questioning is less about the answer and more for the record. The question becomes a point of reference, significant for having been asked. *What did the president know and when did he know it?* Senator Howard Baker famously asked in the middle of the Watergate hearings. The question led to damning testimony that put Richard Nixon squarely in the middle of the cover-up. For-the-record questions can be retrieved, replayed, and revisited as a snapshot in time, a moment of accountability.

The Audience: Confrontational questioning is often directed as much at the audience—a jury, a review board, the general public—as it is at the individual. Use your questions to articulate and illustrate acceptable versus unacceptable behavior. Draw the line in the sand. Even if you do not elicit much new information, your questions can focus attention and get noticed.

The Risk: Confrontational questions can be dangerous. They don't build bridges, they often destroy them. Ask these questions carefully, deliberately. Calculate and be sure you're right. Falsely accusing someone can kill your credibility, make you look foolish and empower your adversary. Whether a brutal dictator or a rebellious teenager, a certain swagger flows from having survived a challenge and defied authority.

Listen: When you ask about wrongdoing, listen for evasive or distracting language or words that change the subject or shift blame. Listen for uncomfortable silences that suggest someone is searching for just the right words. If you hear that, pounce. Listen for a shred of admission, revelation, or remorse. That's when you lean in and ask more.

Try: Attempt some confrontational questioning. A college student stands accused of plagiarism. She turned in a paper on dying coral reefs. She is a solid student and has never been in trouble, but a plagiarism app revealed whole sections of the paper lifted from Wikipedia—word for word. A committee will hear the case. You're the prosecuting professor. Write ten questions. Make them short and precise, each focused on a specific element of the allegation. Do not ask flatly if the student admits to the charge. Build the case a step at a time.

CREATIVITY QUESTIONS

Creativity questions encourage people to think about things that go beyond the familiar. They encourage originality and risk-taking. They ask people to consider new ideas and imagine new scenarios. They put us in the future tense. They push boundaries. Creativity questions ask people to imagine ambitiously and think independently.

The Dream: What would you change? What if there were no limits? What is your dream?

These are opening questions that grant license and unleash the imagination. You are asking people to put convention to the side, to set their sights high and try something new or experiment. These questions inspire people to think big, over the horizon to imagine new approaches, new definitions. They are the questions that frame the challenge, set the bar, and loosen the rules.

The Frame: What's the next Big Thing? How can we eliminate poverty? What will it take to beat cancer? What's the unexpected twist in the story? Frame your question to inspire and to invoke the future. Ask people to imagine a different and better place. Make the questions inspirational, to shift our gaze from the weeds to the sky.

Role-Playing: What if you were CEO? What would you do? What if you were the director making the movie? What would Jeff Bezos think about this situation? Ask your collaborators to try on another pair of shoes—the shoes of the decision maker. Ask them to assume responsibility. Your question puts them in another place. Now they are invested, thinking in a different context and imagining at another level.

Your Sunglasses: When should you take them off? You can direct the action and tell people precisely when to take off their sunglasses or you can ask people to invest themselves in the decision and think about what they are doing, why and to what effect? Invite them to be part of the creative process instead of just handing them a script. These questions challenge people to take ownership of the script and the creative process.

Time Travel: You succeeded. You're in the future. What are you doing? What's it like? What do you see? Skip past the particulars, the details, and the distractions. Forget the fear and the can't-do white noise. Pretend money doesn't exist. Ask people to boldly go where no one has gone before: the future. Ask them to look around and try it on. Then look in the rearview mirror to see how you got there and what it took.

The Superhero: What would you do if you knew you could not fail? That's Gavin Newsom's question. Ask it to help people embrace risk and understand that fear of failure should not stand in the way of brainstorming, big ideas, and worthy goals.

Listen: Be alert to the brave and the different, and for ideas that spark imagination and enthusiasm. Listen eagerly for originality and boldness. If you hear a germ of an idea, fascinating but not fully developed, draw it out with a series of questions that nurture the thought process.

Try: Run the "future test" with a roomful of colleagues, friends, or family. It is five years from now. We achieved our goal. What does that look like? What are we doing? What are we proud of? The questions are about the future but asked and answered in the present tense. The future is now. Your time machine worked.

MISSION QUESTIONS

Mission questions ask us to find shared purpose and turn a challenge into a common goal. They ask us how we can contribute and accomplish something worthy and needed. These questions connect mission to people. They inspire generosity and help us come together, give of ourselves, and accomplish good things.

Discovery: What do you care about? What do you stand for? What are your passions in life?

Start by asking about what matters and why. If a friend is interested in childhood obesity, find out why. If they're passionate about global hunger, is it because they were in the Peace Corps and helped feed a village or because they have been to New Delhi and witnessed hunger up close? Discover the mission and understand where it comes from.

Aspirations and Mission: Once you've established motivation and purpose, you can ask what your friend wants to do or change. What difference does she want to make? Where has she directed her efforts and to what result? Does she know what you are doing and how it aligns with her interests? These questions help you find the pieces you share and the places you complement each other.

Join Forces: How can you work together to advance the cause? How would your common goals be advanced if you joined forces? Look ahead and ask what you can accomplish together. What roles will you play? What's needed most? What will you have to show for your efforts? What difference will it make? Whether in philanthropy or in a mission-driven workplace, these are the questions that flesh out shared purpose and establish aspirations and goals.

Listen: Carefully listen for expressions of interest in a cause, a problem or a mission-driven job. Take special note of personal anecdotes or stories that bring the mission to life or examples of past activities that could indicate areas for collaboration. Pick up on comments that suggest your interests overlap and your goals are similar.

Try: A brain sharpener. Sit with a friend for half an hour and ask about his or her volunteer work or philanthropy. Don't take notes, but find five related convictions or activities that you share. Now ask a series of questions about each. This exercise will force you to ask targeted questions and listen intently. It's also a memory test. Be genuinely interested in the other person. Again, try to have this conversation without using the words "I" or "me."

SCIENTIFIC QUESTIONS

Asking through a science lens starts with a question, which becomes a hypothesis you can test. This involves observation, experimentation, and measurement—and trying to prove your hypothesis wrong. Answers to these questions are building blocks, which often raise more questions along the way, allowing you to explore the unknown. This process brings data and discipline to your discovery.

Observation: What do you see? What do you know? What are you trying to explain? Observe and define the problem you want to solve. Look around. Wonder aloud. Then craft the question.

Hypothesis: You know that more widgets sell in the afternoon, but why? Your hypothesis: More widgets sell in the afternoon because people get paid in the morning. Keep your hypothesis crisp and logical. Write it down. Come back to it. It forms the basis of what you are trying to prove or disprove.

The Data: How much, how fast, how big, how far? Ask what you need to measure and how you can do it over time. Try it. Do an experiment. Collect numbers—the data. Ask if you can replicate the data. Then do it again to see if your findings hold up. Are they supporting or contradicting your hypothesis?

The Contrarian: What disproves or contradicts your hypothesis? What evidence argues against it? Why? You went into this exercise knowing that the only way your hypothesis holds up is if you cannot prove it wrong. So ask the toughest questions. Question the data. Where did it come from? What's weak, what's inconsistent, what doesn't hold up? If you can't disprove your hypothesis, you might actually be onto something.

Conclusion: What does the data prove? How does it answer the question you started with? What's next? Review your question, your hypothesis, your evidence, and your areas of uncertainty, and then you can draw a conclusion. Share it with other smart people and ask them what they think. Where do they see problems? What have you missed? Does your conclusion hold up?

Onward: Now what? What's the next thing I want to figure out? Like all good science, one piece of knowledge builds on another and invites the next. Having answered the question you started with, what is the next question to ask?

Listen: Pay attention to the data. Listen to what is real and can be measured, seen, heard, felt. Listen for hints that your hypothesis is off target, misguided, or flat-out wrong. If it is, start again.

Try: Ask a what's-going-on-here question and then come up with a hypothesis about what causes or complicates the situation. Now figure out how to test your hypothesis over a finite period of time. Think of three ways you will try to prove yourself wrong. Write those reasons down and put them someplace you'll see them every day.

INTERVIEW QUESTIONS

Job interview questions look into the future. They try to predict whether skills and personalities will be a fit. They examine past performance as an indicator of future results. Interview questions are compatibility questions. People who are good at asking them make better interviewers and applicants alike.

Calling Card: What do you like about what you do? This is an open-ended question that may sound like small talk but illuminates big pieces of someone's interests and personality. "Tell me about yourself" can prompt answers about how someone thinks and how she expresses herself.

The Accomplishment: What are you proudest of? What's the wildest idea you have turned into reality? Asking about achievement should elicit discussion about examples and details, interests and capabilities. These questions don't invite bragging; they offer an opportunity to talk about accomplishment and follow-through.

The Challenge: What's the biggest setback you've had and what did you do about it?

Ask about setbacks, shortcomings, failure, and lessons learned. These questions reality-check for humility. They ask about someone's willingness to take risks. They can prompt instructive stories about adversity and resilience.

Goals: What motivates you? What are you trying to achieve? If you could fix one thing in the world, what would it be? Explore the big picture. Is someone looking for a safe harbor or embarking on an adventure? What role does mission play? How important are values—and do they align with what you're trying to do?

The Curveball: What American city would you give to New Zealand and why? Curveball questions often come sailing in out of the blue. They can be fun or a little weird. Their purpose is to prompt answers that provide a glimpse of spontaneity, creativity, humor, and the ability to deal with the unexpected.

Tough Choices: You have to cut 15 percent of your budget. What do you do? Where do you start? Questions that present a hypothetical situation allow you to see how someone works through a difficult decision or approaches and solves a problem. You'll see if you approve or have a suddenly uneasy feeling.

The Dilemma: You're on deadline but think you may not have enough time to finish the project the way you'd like. How do you proceed? These questions probe the thought process behind difficult decision-making.

Your Turn: What do you consider the biggest threat and the biggest opportunity? What are you trying to achieve? How creative can I be? Job candidates should do their homework and take great questions into their interview. Be specific. Ask about the organization, its strengths and its challenges; about the culture, metrics and what motivates the enterprise. Ask what is valued and what is needed. These questions allow the candidate to show interest and demonstrate both knowledge and curiosity.

Listen: Listen to see if the person comes across as direct or disjointed, uncertain or confident. When you ask about common goals and shared values is the answer comfortable and convincing? Listen for stories, examples, reflections, and lessons learned. Listen for expectations because if they don't align, you have a problem.

Try: Write three examples of what you have accomplished in the past and what you aspire to do in the future. Now write two questions about each and answer them out loud. Listen to yourself. Were your answers honest, informative and interesting? Would you hire you?

ENTERTAINING QUESTIONS

Entertaining, three-course questions spice up conversation and bring out the interesting and the fascinating. Fun, irreverent, or probing, these questions can be served up in healthy portions around the table or in the office to help people connect, engage, and learn more about one another. Ask these questions well and you're the master of your own ceremonies!

The Theme:

What is the one thing in the world that blows you away?

This is how you set the theme and steer the conversation. Start with a question that will intrigue and engage everyone. Ask in a way that is not threatening or intimidating. Frame the question so everyone can chime in somehow—with an experience or an opinion, a factual observation, or a personal story. You can make the theme question serious or fun, big or little.

Riddles: If we went to Mars, what would change? If you had three wishes, what would the second one be? What will be the big breakthrough of the next twenty years?

These are game-show questions, imagination starters. You're asking people to weigh in on a riddle that has no right or wrong answer. But in answering, they reveal some of their thinking and personality. These are brainteasers, guaranteed to produce surprises along the way.

Trendsetters: What happens when two-year-olds have smartphones? What would it take for you to buy an autonomous vehicle? Why should we still teach handwriting?

Really? Trends provoke thought and commentary about our time and condition. Questions like these capture the zeitgeist and the human dynamic. They intrigue, surprise, amuse, and captivate. Ask about the present and the future. Invite your guests to close their eyes and imagine.

The News: Is America still capable of doing great things? How will China change the world? What will it take for the home team to win the World Series?

A three-course question gains caloric content if the stakes are real and some people in the room actually *know* something about it. Ask about the world. Look at your guest list for the gold mines of interesting experience or expertise. These questions make headlines and invite people to talk, think, learn, debate, and disagree.

Supper with Socrates: What is success? Do you need success to be successful? Is success always good? Is it a virtue?

Pick an issue or an attribute. Ask a series of poignant questions to pick it apart, define, and debate it. Challenge conventional wisdom, standing definitions, and just about anything that people take for granted. Ask what is true, how we know, why we care. Steer people away from the personal or anecdotal and toward fact, reason, and experience. This could go deep—or just plain exasperate. So keep the conversation focused, bringing participants back to the core questions. This is some of the most thought-provoking stuff you can serve up.

Laugh: What's your most embarrassing experience? If you could erase one day in your life, which day . . . and why? If you made a commercial, what would you be selling?

Questions that point at ourselves show that we don't take ourselves so seriously. Asking for the funniest, weirdest, or most unexpected can prompt a laugh or entertain a crowd.

Listen: These questions can delight or they can ruin your party. Listen to keep the conversation moving and amazing. But also listen for hints of annoyance, resentment, or impatience. Some topics, framed the wrong way, can be poisonous—religion, politics, money come to mind. You need the right crowd and the right host to come in for a soft landing. Listen to determine when you should exercise the host's prerogative to change the subject.

Try: Select questions as you'd select a meal: appetizers, a main course, and dessert. Make note of the interests and experiences your guests bring to the party. Pick your courses accordingly, starting with something light, moving into the stuff you can sink your teeth into, and ending with something sweet. Don't overdo it. Let it breathe. Leave room for coffee.

LEGACY QUESTIONS

Legacy questions ask about what we've done, the people we've touched, and the contributions we've made. They can be asked every day, at every stage. They help recognize accomplishment, express gratitude, set priorities, or fill a bucket list. They help us recognize what is significant and what matters.

Accomplishments: What are the most important things you've done? What are you proud of? Asking what you have accomplished, whom you have helped, what you have created is a powerful way of taking stock and seeing your own footprint. These questions identify accomplishments and contributions.

Appreciation: What do you want your great grandchildren to know about you? Ask yourself this: if a stranger read your biography, what would she say were the significant things you've done? Fresh eyes may see more clearly than your own the contributions you've made along the way.

Adversity: What is a lesson you'd share from a mistake you made? Ask about adversity, mistakes, and regrets. Most everyone will have a clock they'd turn back, but mistakes can be redemptive. These questions seek meaning in mistakes by asking what we've learned from them and how we've used them to teach others. Asking about the downside in this way has an upside.

The Bucket List: What's an adventure you'd like to go on? What do you want to do most? What's your unfinished business? These questions ask you to daydream. You probably won't do it all, but your bucket can become a road map, a way to focus on the future, on the things that matter and the story you're writing.

Ending Questions: How do you want to be remembered? Speaking of story, who is the character you want to be? These questions cut through all the others. Time's up. Book's done. What do you want the title to be? What do you want on the inside flap? How do you want the critics to write about you? How do you want the story to unfold?

Listen to Your Own Voice: Listen for nuggets of accomplishment, expressions of pride, gratitude and satisfaction. Pick up on names and ask more about each. Listen for the high notes and pursue them. Listen for regrets and ask what lessons they taught.

Try: Set up a time to speak with a family member, making clear that you want to ask about significant moments, experiences and people. Prepare your questions in "clusters" so you have several that flow from the first. For example: What's the most significant, yet challenging, relationship you've ever had? Ask follow-ups from the cluster, corresponding to what you just heard. Tell me more. Where did you meet? What was this person like? Why significant? How were you similar? How were you different? What was the best day you had together? The toughest? The point here is to ask in series—half a dozen questions or more per cluster—to dig in deliberately and listen intently in search of recollection, meaning and the defining stories of life.

INDEX

INDEX

ABOUT THE AUTHOR

FRANK SESNO is an Emmy Award–winning journalist and interviewer with more than thirty years of experience reporting from around the world. Well known for his work as anchor, White House correspondent, and talk-show host on CNN, he continues to engage with some of the world's leading personalities as a nationally renowned moderator and through the Conversation Series at The George Washington University.

Frank has interviewed five U.S. presidents, international heads of state, business leaders, and a wide array of globally influential figures throughout his career.

Frank currently serves as director of The George Washington University's School of Media and Public Affairs, where he works with a world-class faculty and teaches classes on journalism ethics, documentary, sustainability reporting, and the art of the interview. He continues to appear on CNN, NPR, and in other media, discussing journalism, politics, and current events. In 2008, Frank launched planetforward.org, where people tell stories to inspire the future.